WHY FOUR GOSPELS?

WHY FOUR GOSPELS?

Donald Bridge

Mentor

Acknowledgements
My wife Rita typed the opening chapters of this book, often whilst accompanying me on missions or at conventions. Mrs. Brenda Baxter keyed much of it into her word processor in her own home – often whilst under much pressure. To both of them, I am very grateful indeed. Thank you!

ISBN 1-85792-225-5
Published in 1996

Mentor
is an imprint of
Christian Focus Publications,
Geanies House, Fearn, Ross-shire,
Scotland, IV20 1TW, Great Britain.
Cover design by Donna Macleod

CONTENTS

INTRODUCTION

This book grew out of an earlier one. Each is complete in itself, and either one can be read before the other.

In *Jesus – The Man and His Message*, I attempted a portrait of Jesus the supreme communicator. Placing his words and actions against the background of his own time and culture (first century Judaism) I tried to explain how it was that even his enemies were compelled to acknowledge that no-one else ever spoke like this man.

I soon realised that a sequel, or at least a complementary view was necessary. For my unspoken and unargued assumption was that a uniform and consistent picture of 'what Jesus was like' can be reconstructed from the New Testament evidence. Yet that material is drawn from four different books that each give a different and distinctive impression.

The differences are striking, significant, illuminating – and sometimes disconcerting. The Four Gospels may not be as different as chalk from cheese (in the words of an old proverb). But they are certainly as distinct as white, green, yellow and purple chalk ... or Cheddar, Stilton and Red Leicester cheese.

The 1960s musical *Jesus Christ, Superstar* cheerfully imagines Matthew, Mark, Luke and John sitting in one room and agreeing to write four Gospels. Of course, it was not like that. But what *was* it like, and why did they do it?

Why do Matthew and Luke give completely different accounts of Christ's birth, whilst John settles for a profound discussion of its meaning, and Mark does not so much as mention it? Why are the 'seven sayings from the cross' scattered across all four Gospels? Why does John's Jesus sound so different from Matthew's? The pursuit of these questions (I find) becomes a fascinating journey of discovery and faith.

Let me be clear: I am not a scholar; only a student. I managed to reach the minimum standard of study required for the ordained ministry. Later, I spent a memorable summer sabbatical learning the elements of biblical archaeology in Jerusalem. Later again, I lived and worked as a chaplain in Jerusalem, and criss-crossed Judaea and Galilee for fourteen months, in search of clues and insights.

Apart from that, my knowledge of the Gospels is essentially a working knowledge. Their contents have worked within me and shaped my life for sixty-five years. They have informed and directed my preaching for fifty. I constantly see what they *do*, as well as hear what they *say*.

Biblical scholarship, of course, has its place. The research and thinking of others has often enlightened my understanding, often engaged my faith, and sometimes challenged my prejudices! The fact that I only quote a few scholars is not an indication that I only read a few. No-one with a library ticket for Durham University and another in Jerusalem is likely to make that mistake! Nevertheless, this book simply describes how a plain man who ministers to plain people is learning to see the Four Gospels.

If the reading of this book sends a hundred Christians back to read those masterpieces of condensation with a new enthusiasm, I shall be pleased. If it opens ten lives to the Christ who walks today's world as surely (if not as physically) as he strode the lanes of Galilee, I shall taste the joy again that I have tasted so often before; that of saying, 'Mr. Jones ... Mrs. Smith ... meet the Master!'

Donald Bridge
Kirby-le-Soken,
Essex, Great Britain
1996

Looking at
Four Portraits

Chapter 1

INVITATION TO A JOURNEY

At various times in the second half of the first century four men sat down in different parts of the Roman Empire and wrote a few thousand words each. What they wrote would change the history of mankind. The joint effect of their four booklets, each about the length of a modern tabloid newspaper, is still increasing and unfolding to this day. It permeates the societies of this planet like yeast working in a batch of dough – exactly as they said it would. Their names have been anglicised as Matthew, Mark, Luke and John. They wrote what have been known ever since as *the Four Gospels*.

We know little about those men. None of them put his name to what he wrote. We are not sure of the language they used. We can only guess where their four localities were: one theory suggests Lebanon, Italy, Israel and Turkey. But their readers have been all mankind.

The American preacher Talmage once met the Victorian Englishman, Spurgeon. 'I read your sermons,' said Spurgeon warmly to Talmage. 'The world reads yours' was the reply! Given a little Yankee exaggeration, that was almost true. Say it of the Four Gospels and it is no exaggeration: the world reads them and has done so for twenty centuries.

Their influence is immeasurable. They wrote for a public which did very little private reading, yet their work was quickly hailed as a message from God, throughout Europe and the Middle East, and perhaps as far as India.

In an age when every section had to be copied laboriously by hand and a world bestseller might number five hundred copies, these documents were copied in astonishing numbers.

One estimate suggests sixty thousand copies by the end of the second century.[1]

The movement which these writings stimulated and informed, successfully resisted the most arrogant and powerful political dictatorship the world had so far known, exhausted its hostility and reshaped its life. When that empire eventually crumbled and fell and a new 'dark age' descended, it was those who went on copying and distributing the Gospels who kept light and hope alive until the sparks blazed into life again and once again transformed people who were sunk in savagery, superstition and ignorance.

It was a story to be repeated through the ages. It still happens before our eyes today. When in the early 1990s Mongolia broke free from the Russian Communist clutch, her new rulers adopted the Gospel of Luke as the basis for ethical teaching in primary schools. The American film *Jesus* is based closely on that same Luke's Gospel. By 1994 it had been printed in 6,300 film-copies, dubbed in 250 languages, and shown in 197 countries. It has been watched by 503 million viewers, of whom 33 million have responded with the expressed desire to become Christians.[2] Could these four writers have imagined this as they sharpened their simple pens, mixed their clumsy inks, and unrolled their first pieces of scroll?

Modern Britain is reputed to be post-Christian, the message of Jesus abandoned or ignored, and his name a mere term of blasphemous abuse. Yet interest in the Gospels (which provide our only source of certain information about him) remains intense. Why otherwise would bizarre reconstructions or blatant denials of his story attract such attention? In 1994 a Bible translation society and a university student movement combined to make half a million copies of Luke's Gospel

---

1. Quoted by B.F. Westcott, *A General History of the Canon of the New Testament*, 1875, p. 4. He refers to 'Mr. Norton's calculations' in an 1847 book *The Genuineness of the Gospels*. Westcott describes 'large cheap editions published in Rome'.
2. Figures published by Campus Crusade, 1994.

available in colleges throughout Britain. The assumption was that interest, discussion and debate would be stirred wherever the booklet was offered. So it proved to be.

Why is the most famous help-agency for the depressed and suicidal called *Samaritans*? Luke's Gospel tells us. Why is the phrase 'no room at the inn' so expressive of rejection and marginalization? Same answer. Why are people who have learned a bitter lesson the hard way called 'returning prodigals'? Luke again.

Lives transformed

Something more important than language and folklore is found here – more important ultimately than the opinions of the great, too. The fact is that in every generation since Nero fiddled, countless numbers of ordinary men and women have found themselves confronted and transformed by the Figure of whom Matthew and his three friends speak and write.

In the 1990s the Bishop of Chester celebrated the history of his cathedral by organizing the distribution of the Gospel of John to every household in his diocese. He expressed the conviction that few people who were prepared to read the pocket booklet with an open mind could get past chapter ten without committing their lives and souls to Jesus Christ. That is my experience too. More times than I can number I have engaged an impromptu audience at a marketplace, fairground or racecourse and have finished my talk with the free offer of a copy of that same Gospel. Often the consequence, days or weeks later, has been conviction and conversion.

I recall a professional thief at Chester Races. He was drunk when he accepted the booklet and was puzzled when, next morning, he found it in his raincoat pocket. Idle curiosity led him to read it. He came to faith in Christ. When the preachers of the Open Air Mission met him years later, he was a deacon in a Baptist Church – and he was allowed to take the collection without one hand tied behind his back!

As I write, a tabloid newspaper features an article on the supposed unreliability of the Gospel record.[3] An armchair specialist seems to have recently discovered some long-since exploded theories of nineteenth-century German critics, and trots them out as – well, gospel truth. According to him, the Christmas star never shone, the wise men never moved, the parables were never told and the first Christians never meant to say the Easter tomb was empty. The Gospels, he assures us, are full of ridiculous and obvious self-contradictions. The only real mystery to readers of the article must be how such a bunch of bunglers managed to produce something that has convinced the minds and changed the lives of millions!

Roots of our language
The great of today's world frequently quote these ancient, allegedly disproved booklets. Mikhail Gorbechov often appealed to them as he began the unthinkable task of dismantling Soviet communism. Nelson Mandela quoted them as he led an African subcontinent into astonishing moral and social change. Margaret Thatcher appealed to them for support of her economic policies (perhaps with more ingenuity than accuracy!). Twenty years earlier the very world of pop-music that was busy promoting permissiveness nevertheless felt obliged to produce re-interpretations of the Gospel story – *Jesus Christ Superstar* and *Godspell* being the most famous.

The very language of English (now an almost universal language) is permeated with word pictures and idiomatic phrases from these books. 'Turn the other cheek', 'Judge not', 'seek and you will find', 'let your light shine', 'watch and pray', 'get behind me, Satan', 'kingdom come', 'pearls before swine', 'a great gulf fixed', the examples multiply almost indefinitely. Hidden in our own language, their origin often forgotten but their power of communication undimmed, the words of Mark and his colleagues permeate our speech.

---

3. Article by Enoch Powell, MP, in *The Daily Mail*, 20 August, 1994.

What the Gospels mean to me

This book offers an unashamedly biased and unapologetically personal view of these marvellous and mysterious books. When I say 'biased' I mean that I am personally committed to them as divinely inspired. I do not submit them to my judgment, but rather submit myself to theirs. If that stance is labelled 'traditionalist', 'conservative' or even 'fundamentalist' then so be it. For me it is a matter not of labels but of submission to the One who claims lordship of my faith and obedience. Their language was woven into my childhood. Their teaching I rejected in my teens – until I found myself captured by the towering figure of Jesus who is the centre of their story. Ever since then, their words have intrigued me, informed me, puzzled me, persuaded me, daunted me, yet attracted me. I have no idea how often I have read them from beginning to end. I have expounded them to thousands of people and seen hundreds of lives changed as I did so.

The marvel of modern travel has enabled me to visit every place mentioned in their pages. The marvel of modern media has enabled me to read, view and hear opinions of scholars on every facet of their teaching. I seek now to share, in simplicity, something of what those four ancient authors have come to mean to me.

That has involved asking questions. How reliable are these books? Do they give us fact, fable, literal history, truth-in-pictures, or a mixture of all four? Why have they been included in the Bible, and what do Christians mean by saying they are inspired words from God? Why are there *four* Gospels? How do we account for the differences and how do we explain the likenesses? Did the authors know each other? What was their motive in writing?

There are questions of interpretation too. These powerful narratives were written in a culture so different from ours, with presuppositions so contrary to ours, that they might as well come from a different planet. What has, say, an English housewife, a Scottish engineer, a Welsh doctor, and an Irish clergyman in the twentieth century got in common with a peasant, a farmer, a soldier or a tax-collector in an obscure outpost of the Roman Empire? What relevance can there be in the story of a wandering preacher and healer two millennia ago, in today's age of telecommunication, keyhole surgery, space exploration and nuclear energy? How do I bridge the gap between the ages and find direction, light and life in today's moral maze from a few pamphlets written so long ago?

Yet there is a way. It is possible. This writer has just been interrupted by a lengthy telephone call arranging the details of a Mission in a modern English city. The assumption behind that call (held by caller and recipient alike) is that lives will be changed as people are encouraged to look (perhaps for the first time) at the Man from Nazareth whose powerful, appealing, daunting yet strangely attractive figure walks across the chapters of the Gospels and out of their pages into the lives of those who watch and listen, with redeeming and transforming power.

Join me, then, in exploring some of the questions raised and the answers offered by Matthew, Mark, Luke and John.

Join me on a journey. There will be surprises in plenty. We may have to avoid tempting by-paths. There are potholes into which we could easily stumble. But the authors claim to offer us the path to life.

Chapter 2

CAN WE BELIEVE THE GOSPELS?

First we have to ask a question which might shock older Christians. Are there really any facts? Can we point to anything in black-and-white and say, 'This is what Jesus actually said and did'? In other words, *can we trust the Gospel record?*

An earlier generation of Christians would have replied, 'Of course we can; this is the Bible, God's inspired Word.' Today it is very different. Whatever Christians believe, they are surrounded by people fed on a diet of newspapers, paperbacks and television programmes (not to mention scholars' pronouncements and bishops' opinions) that say something very different. Something like this:

> *The only information we have about Jesus has to be quarried with difficulty from the four Gospels. But they are not reliable. They were composed long after the events they purport to describe – by writers strongly biased in his favour. Their stories have 'grown', as we all know that stories do. The writers fed back into the Jesus-events their own developed beliefs and prejudices, turning the simple figure of the Galilean teacher into a miracle-working God-man. They tell us a lot about the beliefs of Christians seventy years later, but very little about the 'real Jesus'.*

That, I think, is a fair summary of popular opinion today, fortified by newspapers and television pundits. Every sentence is in fact highly contentious and theoretical, but if we hear it on television, surely it must be true!

After one such film, characterised by superb photography but highly contentious 'debunking' of the Bible record, fifteen scholars, representing all faiths and none, complained in a public letter that the film contained not one established scholarly fact. But the film will be remembered, not the letter.[1]

So what are we to make of it all?

First, it is worthwhile mentioning that the four Gospels are not the only records (though they are undoubtedly the fullest and most reliable).

The Jewish historian Josephus bears witness.[2] He was the Galilee commander during the uprising against Rome in AD 67. Later changing sides, he rose high in the Roman aristocracy and wrote a great deal of Jewish history in the hope of setting the record straight. We shall look at Josephus more than once in this book. In a famous passage he sets the life and work of Jesus of Nazareth in the biblical time-frame and circumstances. He confirms the crucifixion and admits that many believed Jesus to be the promised Christ. He refers to belief in the resurrection in words that make his own attitude to it equivocal.

The Roman historian Tacitus, writing early in the second century, gives us a factual foundation for our understanding of the first century in Rome.[3] He speaks contemptuously of the early Christians in the capital, but grudgingly acknowledges the persecution they were willing to endure for their faith. He confirms the general outline of the facts, linking the crucifixion with Tiberius the emperor and Pontius Pilate the Judaean governor (exactly as the Bible does). Most impressive of all

---

1. The film was *Jesus – The Evidence*, produced by London Weekend Television as three episodes in April 1994. The third in the series was the episode that earned it widespread condemnation because of its reckless speculation, presented as scholarly opinion.
2. Josephus: *Antiquities* 18:63, 64.
3. Tacitus: *Annals* 15:44.

is his admission that 'the detestable superstition broke out again' in the capital itself. But why and how? Crucifixions were cruelly commonplace. Judaea was an obscure province on the edge of the empire. What are people doing in Rome itself, counting as King an executed carpenter and threatening the interests of a deranged dictator?

Somewhat later, another Roman, Celsus, launched a bitter attack on the early church (known to us because we have some spirited answers from Christian leaders).[4] He reviled the lifestyle of Jesus in twisted but recognisable references to the Sermon on the Mount. He attributed Christ's miracles to black magic, but it never occurred to him to deny that they ever happened. In this he resembles hostile Jewish writers early in the second century. They too bear unintended witness to the powerful effect that Jesus had on people and on movements.

It is worth mentioning, too, the discovery of some 'Sayings of Jesus' in Egypt, during 1946 – part of what is the Nag Hammadi library. They are mixed up with teaching that clearly reflects a second-century heretical sect whose appearance can be traced elsewhere long after the time of Jesus. Nevertheless, many of the 'Gospel sayings' are scattered amongst them (including short versions of eleven of Jesus' parables).[5]

Other biblical witnesses

Another source and confirmation of the Jesus-facts is often forgotten or disregarded. I mean other references in the New Testament writings outside of the four Gospels. Christians often fail to realise that these were written independently of the Gospels and in some cases well before Mark and his colleagues ever put pen to paper. For example, whether Paul is believed or not and whether his writings are accepted as Scripture or not, the fact acknowledged by everyone is that he

---

4. For a popular account of extra-biblical evidence, see *Jesus 2000*, Lion, 1989.
5. Blomberg, pp 208-214.

wrote shortly after the events and could regard them as widely known and undisputed.

An example is Paul's first letter to Thessalonica, written perhaps six months after he planted that European church. A likely date is AD 51, confirmed by references in the letter which can be checked with known history. This letter is full of undesigned confirmations. Paul is simply referring to what he and his converts knew and believed *within eighteen years of the crucifixion*. Jesus is pictured as a known figure, his teaching constantly echoed, his death and resurrection proclaimed, his promised return anticipated.

Let me quote one significant reference: his return will be like that of 'a thief in the night' (an extraordinary and puzzling simile). But Paul has not invented it. Years later, Jesus' words would be recorded by Matthew and Luke – and years later again by Peter.[6]

The same kind of references can be drawn from Paul's letter to the Galatians (written either 51 or 57) and to the Romans (57). The earliest verses of Romans, for example, assume that Jesus was a Jewish descendant of King David and that his resurrection declared him to be the Son of God – all this before Matthew took up his pen to prove exactly that. Then where did the ideas come from?

Even more striking is evidence in the little letter of James. Josephus tells us a lot about this 'brother of Jesus', his lifestyle, influence and death. Every indication of the man's own writing is very early indeed: Christians still meet in synagogues for example, and there is not a suggestion of Gentile converts (James 1:1 and 2:2; 'synagogues' is not used in some translations, but that is what James meant). A date as early as 48-50 seems likely – and 42 is possible – *perhaps ten*

---

6. Paul at Thessalonica: Acts 17 and 18; 1 Thessalonians 1-3. Gallio was proconsul of Corinth, AD 51-52, according to an inscription discovered in Delphi. References to 'a thief in the night' are 1 Thessalonians 5:2; Matthew 24:43-44; Luke 12:39-40; 2 Peter 3:10.

years after the crucifixion, and several years before any of the Gospels. What is most striking about this letter is the constant, undeliberate, half-conscious reflection of Jesus' words in every paragraph. James does not quote them; it is more impressive than that. They have become his own; he simply alludes to them in undesigned coincidences. But how can non-events and unspoken words be woven into the writer's memory?

External evidence
In the previous section we looked inside the Bible. But there is plenty of supportive evidence outside of its pages, and outside of that very Christian community which those pages were shaping. Let me give you some.

First, the Gospel record fits *what we know of the ancient Middle East.*

There is now a huge quantity of information available to picture for us the world of Jesus and his apostles.[7] Much has always been available to examine (like the vast tracts of the Jewish Talmud). More has been discovered (and no doubt still more remains to be unearthed) mouldering on the shelves of ancient monasteries.

One example is the romantic discovery in the early nineteenth century of the *Diatessaron*, a 'harmony of the four Gospels' written in the second century, and often quoted in the third.[8] It lay neglected and 'lost' in the Vatican library. More still has come to light through modern historical research and reconstruction.

And more still again was found in clay jars secreted in Judaean caves for nineteen centuries until their accidental discovery in 1947. Here, with spine-tingling awe, we read documents written when Jesus walked in Galilee, and argu-

---

7. See my *Living in the Promised Land.*
8. *Diatessaron*: a Greek musical term meaning 'four part harmony'. See article under this name in *New International Dictionary of the Christian Church.*

ments debated in his hearing in Jerusalem – the famous Dead Sea Scrolls from Qumran.[9]

All of this knowledge is available on any good library bookshelf. What does it tell us? Little of it directly 'proves' the Gospel story. Much of it indirectly confirms it. In spite of the assertions of some paperback writers with one eye on headlines and the other on royalties, there are few actual references to Jesus (in the Qumran scrolls, none at all). But what they do is all the more impressive for being indirect. They fill in the cultural, religious and social background – and confirm that it was just as the Gospel writers reflect it.

Here are the groups so familiar from the New Testament records: Pharisees (the teachers) and Sadducees (the priests), Herodians (the politicians), Zealots (the Gospel writers refer to them as bandits or insurrectionists). Here are the same public figures, too. We find Annas and Caiaphas sharing the high-priesthood – as wily, worldly and cynically pragmatic on other pages as they are in the New Testament. We come across shifty, power-hungry Pilate, governor of Judaea, and have several anecdotes that explain how he was already in bad trouble for causing unnecessary conflict between the Jewish religion and Roman politics – the very reason why the priests could twist his arm at the trial of Jesus.

The whole climate of opinion is confirmed, too. Bible critics of a liberal kind used to dismiss John's Gospel as a pious fiction from the second century. 'People just didn't talk the way Jesus is supposed to have talked at that time and place,' they said. Wrong! The Dead Sea Scrolls, from precisely Jesus' time and place, are full of those very concepts and those very words.

Clearest of all is the picture of a society constantly buzzing with rumours, agog with expectation, and explosive with speculation about the promised and soon coming Messiah.

---

9. *Dead Sea Scrolls*. See new English translation by Geza Vermes, Penguin, 1994.

Secondly, we have *evidence from the archaeologist's spade.*
The case here is similar to that of historical research. The
archaeologist uncovers artifacts, structures and sites, and then
draws cautious conclusions from them. It is the art (someone
has said unkindly) of digging up rubbish and then writing it
down! In general terms (and sometimes in dramatic particu-
lars) archaeology confirms the Gospel background and even
pinpoints some of the places. John's Gospel in particular reads
almost like a guidebook to Jerusalem between AD 20 and 70
(after which it was destroyed or totally changed). John repeatedly 'gets it right'. I shall return to this fact in a later chapter.

One of the most picturesque examples is the Pool of
Bethesda, where John 5 places Jesus' miracle of healing a lame
man. Once said to be unidentifiable and intended to represent
a mythological truth, it has been discovered and excavated.
There are the five colonnades, there is the nearby sheep-gate,
there is even evidence of a disreputable healing-centre frowned
on by Jewish priests. So what happens to all those neat
explanations of the five porches symbolising the five books of
Moses, and the made-up miracles representing the superiority
of grace over law? It really happened, and we can stand on the
spot!

Look next at *eyewitness accounts.* Any unbiased reading of the
Gospels brings out evidence of personal recollection, especially in Mark and John. You can hear the splash of the sea, the
murmur of the crowds, the astonishment of the disciples. Luke
is rather different. The sense of personal memory is missing.
That is what we should expect, for Luke makes it clear that he
is not an eyewitness; he simply talked to those who were. I was
amused to read recently that Luke has only a tourist's knowledge of Palestine. A tourist is exactly what he was; a Gentile
visitor to the Holy Land, not a native like the others. My
amusement sprang from reflection that the places he specifically mentions are exactly those sites to which I sometimes

take a party of tourists and pilgrims nowadays. Luke shows us
Joppa where Peter had his vision, Roman Caesarea where he
preached in the military compound, the Mount of Olives and
the village of Emmaus with their exact distances from Jerusalem, the Temple area (with its Beautiful Gate, Solomon's
Colonnade and the steps up to the Antonia Fortress). The first
two I usually show people on Day One, and the others on Day
Five of the package-tour!

Coincidence and contradiction provide an added argument. I put these together as evidences for the veracity of the
Gospel accounts. Unintended coincidence is always impressive. A true eyewitness account will record little details that
have no special importance. They are there simply because
that is how it happened, and that is how it is remembered. Quite
coincidentally, they match some other more important facts.
For example, John recalls that five thousand people about to
be miraculously fed, sat down on 'plenty of green grass' (John
6:10). In fact, grass is sparse in the region (the northern rim of
Lake Galilee). It is found in one area, but only for a few weeks
in early Spring (after the Winter rain has had its effect, during
the first rise in Spring temperature that triggers growth, and
before the blazing Summer sun scorches it or the goats eat it).
John also mentions in passing that it was close to Passover time
– in fact, early Spring! The picture 'fits'.

The presence of 'contradiction' proves a similar point.[10]
Different Gospel writers present rather different accounts of
the same event. This can worry Christians, and affords derisive
material for atheistic hecklers in open-air meetings (as I've
noticed). The stories of Jesus' resurrection appearances are
notoriously difficult to put together in a consistent order. But
apparent contradictions are familiar whenever several truthful witnesses tell it as they recall it.

Every court judge knows that; so does every policeman. In

---

10. See my *Jesus, the Man and His Message* (chapter 10) and John
Wenham: *The Easter Enigma*.

fact, if several allegedly independent witnesses gave exactly the same story in every detail, the judge would immediately suspect a cooked-up story. The sure sign of people conspiring to tell a complicated series of lies is this: their story will appear to agree on the surface, but will collapse under careful investigation. Truthful witnesses reveal the very opposite. Their stories appear on the surface to contradict. But after careful investigation the underlying truth emerges with increasing clarity, and apparent contradictions are resolved. That is exactly what happens in the Gospel accounts.

The Ring of Truth. It is simply not true to say that there are no clear and certain facts on which to base a decision about Jesus of Nazareth. Cultural reflections, historical research, archaeological discoveries, eyewitness memories, undesigned coincidences and truthful contradictions: here are the signs that the Gospel records have about them the ring of truth. If we want to find 'the real Jesus', God has given us enough to reward our search. On the result of that search our hope of heaven depends. It matters as much as that.

Chapter 3

WHY FOUR?

We are still asking questions and pursuing clues. No questions could be more important, no quest more urgent. If Jesus is the unique revelation of God and the only way to God as the Gospels say he is, how much can we know about him, and what is it that we know?

And here is an odd fact. We are given, not one account of his life and work, but four. Famous people in the twentieth century are introduced to us by two distinct kinds of book. Some publish their own memoirs (the way skilfully prepared by hints, leaks and propaganda). A little later someone produces an authorised biography. Jesus neither wrote the first nor set in motion the second. The astonishing fact is that he, of whom more books have ever been written than any one else in the history of mankind, never wrote anything himself. If it were not for one incident, we would not even be sure that he could write, however one other incident makes it clear that he could read (John 8:1-11; Luke 4:14-19).

There is, of course, a third way in which celebrities become known. People write *about* them, but not directly *on their behalf*. Such books are usually sketches rather than authorised biographies. They give impressions, from the viewpoint of the writer. A truly great and complex character would need to have several such sketches to do him justice. People have written of Sir Winston Churchill as a product of English society at a certain period; as a climbing politician who espoused seemingly lost causes; as a skilled and eloquent historian with a romantic vision of Britain's greatness; as a painter of some skill; as a Tory scourge of Socialism; as an architect of modern Europe. Most of all, however, he is recorded as a war leader of genius. Each account is 'true' – none alone is the 'whole truth'. The accounts need to supplement each other.

It is, then, hardly surprising that we have several 'sketches' of Jesus. There have been more than four, only four were recognised from the beginning as unique, inspired and authoritative. They are known today as the 'Gospels' of Matthew, Mark, Luke and John.

We might think of them as four portraits of one person. In 1993 five postage stamps were issued to mark the fortieth anniversary of the accession to the throne of Her Majesty, Queen Elizabeth the Second. Each was a delightful miniature of a different portrait of the Queen. We saw her depicted as head of the Commonwealth, head of the Armed Forces, head of the Church of England, head of Parliament, head of the Royal Family. In each she was appropriately dressed for one distinctive role. It would be quite impossible to depict all five roles in one portrait, or on one postage stamp.

Here is one explanation of our Four Gospels. Each was written to bring out some different facet of the glory of Jesus' character and work. How could one suffice? 'Jesus my shepherd, Saviour, friend, my prophet, priest and king', we sing in one of John Newton's hymns. And so much more.

Each writer also addressed himself to a rather different Christian community, and felt the need to do so because of varying circumstances. But the consequence is more important than the cause. For the cause can only be conjectured, but the consequence is a marvellous multi-dimensional picture of Jesus Christ.

Four portraits of one person, then. How do they differ, and in what ways do they complement one another? We can begin with a few simple statements.

Mark addresses Romans (I shall seek to establish that later). They were pragmatic, practical, active realists (which is why they conquered the known world). If someone attracted their attention or made a bid for their loyalty, they would ask a simple question: what did he do? Mark tells us exactly that. In a fast-moving tale, as brief as the report of a modern journalist, he shows Jesus in action. The story is full of verbs and adverbs. It bowls along at an almost breathless pace. This is what happened when Jesus stormed into people's lives, says Mark. Here is the Servant King, the Man for Others, giving himself totally to the transforming of people's situations. There is teaching, too – straight from the lips of Jesus. It sounds blunt, searching, brief, succinct and very straight. This is what Jesus did: he acted and spoke with power.

Matthew speaks to Jews (a hundred clues make that clear). Above all, a Jew asks of anyone, 'Who is he?' Awareness of the call of God to a special people lay at the heart of the Jewish life. So the first questions asked are 'Where does he fit into the story of God's people?' 'Where is he coming from?' 'Who is he?' Matthew tells us. Jesus is a descendant of Abraham, the first Semite to hear God's distinguishing call. He is a descendant of David, Israel's greatest King, to whom was promised a greater to come. The family tree that opens Matthew's book (so unpromisingly to modern Western eyes) tells the Jewish reader what he first wants to know. The drama then unfolds, with the same repeated refrain: 'Who is Jesus?' He is Messiah. He is the focus and fulfilment of all God's promises and purposes. Behold your King, says Matthew.

Luke writes to the great wide world of the Greeks (his style makes that obvious). Himself a cultured and well-read professional, he addresses that pervasive culture which had captured the minds of mankind before the Romans marched, and given everyone a second language. The Greeks asked of anyone who bid for their attention: 'What was he like?' Luke tells us. In a style close to that of the classical historians, he gives us the *bio* of Jesus – his 'life' (see page 32). With deft touches of his brush, he paints a landscape rather than a portrait, a montage rather than a photograph. Jesus is forever impacting people's lives with his actions and words; always intervening to dispel doubt, explode prejudice and change situations. Most of all he is the Man for People. Fictional characters on the margin of acceptability crowd his parables: the Good Samaritan, the Prodigal Son, the folk who excused themselves from the party, the widow who pestered the magistrate for justice. But real people also crowd the pages and they too are the marginalised. Mary Magdalene of the doubtful reputation; Peter the argumentative fisherman; Zacchaeus the shady government official; the leper who could not be touched – these are the people who met him, and this is what they found him to be like says Luke. Jesus is the Saviour of mankind.

John writes to the emerging Christian world. Here is mature theological reflection from a man who lived close by the Master's side in simple Galilee. But he also heard Christ take on the theologians of Jerusalem in subtle dialectic, and match the earnest speculations of the Qumran community. And he lived long enough, did John, to influence far-off Roman Asia and resist the insinuating influences of oriental mysticism; all in the name of Jesus whom he knew to be the Son of God. The question posed by so many as the Church built a life for itself, in the sinful, sophisticated, subtle world of the East, was 'Why did Jesus come?' The reason, John tells us, was to bring men and women to the life-giving knowledge of God, through his life, death, resurrection and indwelling presence.

What did he do? asks Mark – and tells us.
Who was he? poses Matthew – and gives us a clear answer.
What was he like? enquires Luke – and describes his life and ways.
Why did he come? asks John – and gives us the deepest reason.

Who were the readers?

Each pen-portrait was addressed to specific readers, too. One of the helpful contributions of modern scholars is to pose the question, 'To whom did the Evangelists write and what were their circumstances?' Here, apart from those generalities of 'Roman, Jew, Greek and Christian', we are on less sure ground. The Gospel writers, unlike the authors of some of the New Testament letters, never tell us in so many words who they are addressing. Luke and John oblige us by explaining why: the first because he wants a newly instructed convert to be sure of the basic facts; the second because he wants to provide the church with an evangelistic tool (Luke 1:1-4; John 20:30-31).

I want to return to this subject later. It is important. Are we to imagine the four writers working together like Gilbert and Sullivan or (better analogy!) the contributors to a Scripture Union magazine? Almost certainly not. Was the earliest Gospel available to the others? Almost certainly (see my next chapter). How much of what they wrote was original? Why do modern scholars keep referring to 'oral traditions'? What exactly is a Gospel book anyway? A biography? A history book? A theological essay? An evangelistic booklet?

A question of style

In order to understand any piece of writing, we need to have some idea of what is called the *genre*. Does the style adopted by the author help us to see how he expects his work to be understood? Someone who writes poetry does not mean it to 'read' as history. John Buchan wrote his *Thirty-nine Steps* in the first person, but he would not want it to be confused with his autobiography! Although Macbeth was a historical figure, Shakespeare's play of that name is certainly not accurate history, but drama. The soap-opera *Neighbours* is not intended to be a sociological report on Australian life!

The Bible is written in many different styles: one can find the genres of saga, poetry, drama, symbol, parable, personal letter, theological tract, and so on. Our understanding of these various passages partly depends on the kind of writing we believe each to be. So what genres do we recognise in the Gospels?

At first sight, they seem to fit the category of *biography*, for they tell us the story of a real person. But there are problems here. A biography is a very modern thing. It normally opens with a history of the subject's parents and grandparents, and gives detailed information about the 'times' into which he or she was born. It then explores areas like private psychology, influences felt, personal development, motivation and purposes. There are verbal and visual snapshots from childhood and teens, and impressions shared by observers. The Gospel records contain very little of this kind of thing, which springs from a modern outlook on personality.

Of course, prominent people in the ancient world were 'written up' by admirers or biographers, and the result was sometimes called a *bio* (that is, a *life*). This usually took the form of collected anecdotes, grouped according to topic rather than chronology. Marvellous portents surrounding the birth were often a feature, and deathbed scenes (or fatal battles!) were popular. As I pointed out on page 29, the attentive Gospel reader will notice some of these features, especially in Luke, the only non-Jewish Gospel writer.

What I think of as *holy narrative* has a more Jewish precedent. It often appears in the Old Testament, in the great sagas of Abraham and the patriarchs, and then again in the stories of the action-prophets, like Elijah, Elisha and Amos. These were set in known historical periods, from which modern archaeology provides striking confirmation. Matthew and John deliberately invoke this comparison, by presenting Jesus as the 'fulfilment' of these biblical narratives.

There is also a large element of *commentary and interpretation* in the Gospels. At times this is obvious: the writer interrupts himself to remark that Jesus spoke with more authority than the rabbis (Matthew 7:29), that he knew his opponents' true motives (Mark 2:8), that he was determined to go to Jerusalem to face suffering (Luke 9:51-53), and that he knew what the saving consequences of his death would be (John 12:32). At other times the comment is more subtle. It is found under the surface, in the way that each writer marshals his facts, groups his incidents and shapes individual stories to give a particular impression. Modern scholarship, though given at times to unhelpful speculation, has nevertheless done a real service in drawing attention to this.

For example, Mark omits Jesus' last words from the cross, and ends the account with the dreadful 'My God, my God, why have you forsaken me?' (Mark 15:34). In contrast, John makes it clear that the final words were 'It is finished' (John 19:30). What are they telling us? Does Mark want suffering Christians to dwell on the darkness that their Saviour endured? Does John want his readers rather to revel in a work completed for our salvation? And why does Matthew choose differently again, with a loud wordless cry that is followed by the tearing of the great temple curtain that hid the Holy Place? What we are looking at here is inspired interpretation, which invites the reader to search and worship.

This leads to yet another category. I like to call it *living theology*. For example, the Birth Narratives of Matthew and Luke have the same purpose as the more overtly doctrinal prologue of John. All three teach the Incarnation; that God took our humanity and 'dwelt among us'. The Passion Narratives of all four teach the Atonement (Christ died for our sins) as clearly as do the Epistle to the Romans or the Letter to the Hebrews.

What do we have then? The Four Gospels can be described as *dramatic narrative*. Each writer collects incidents and sayings in dramatic form which creates atmosphere, the clash of characters and the tension of colliding events. But each Gospel is also a theological interpretation of Jesus, designed

to elicit faith, nourish Christian living, and explore the meaning of salvation. Each evangelist organises and displays his
material with a number of clear purposes in mind. Each writer
presents a challenge and demands a verdict. Like Pontius
Pilate (although with a very different motive) each says,
'Behold the man' and 'What will you do with Jesus?'

All of this I find fascinating. All of it is involved in asking
'Why four Gospels?' But some suggested answers must await
a more urgent task. If what we have here, beyond and behind
the writers, their readers and their circumstances, is *God's
witness to his Son*, then the first necessity is to listen to that
witness. For, says John, you and I are the ultimate readers to
whom the record is addressed.

> But these are written that you may believe that Jesus is the
> Christ, the Son of God, and that by *believing* you may have
> life in his name (John 20:31).

Each writer of the fourfold witness appeals to you and to me.
What will we make of this Man of whom they write? The leader
of the Roman, the Messiah of the Jew, the Saviour of the Greek
and the Lord of the Church is – what? – to you and me? He
lays claim to the title of Saviour and Lord (Rescuer and
Manager, in our modern parlance) of all. Belgian and Brazil-
ian, Eskimo and Ecuadorian, African and Asian, Scandinavian
and Scot – extend it as far as you can think or imagine – the
Gospels press that claim upon all.

So now we put off these fascinating 'how, who, why and
when?' questions for a few chapters. Before returning to them,
we dare to let the records speak for themselves. This is more
important. Nothing could possibly matter more than this.

Mark

Chapter 4

MARK'S JOURNEY INTO LIFE

I envy the reader who approaches Mark for the first time. Here is a vivid narrative that rattles along at a breathless pace. Here is journalism at its best. Here are unforgettable pen-pictures executed with a few deft strokes. Mark's Gospel is, by any definition, one of the most memorable documents from the ancient world.

To prepare this chapter I read it again at one sitting. I chose a newly published pocket-size edition, bound together with a re-issue of the evangelistic booklet called *A Journey into Life*.[1] How appropriate, for Mark's Gospel is the *first evangelistic booklet of the early church*. And it does indeed describe two journeys: one taken by the Son of God to the cross, and the one taken by the believing reader into true life in Christ. It took me just one hour to read it: it has taken the world two millennia to explore its riches.

Good news in the city

Very strong tradition puts the writing of Mark in Rome. Much of this is due to a curious character called Papias. He was bishop or pastor of the church in Heirapolis, a city not far from Ephesus in today's Turkey, whose early planting was referred to by the apostle Paul (Colossians 4:13). Around the year 110, he seems to have written a five-volume compendium of anecdotes and sayings about Jesus entitled *The Words of Jesus Explained*. This has disappeared, but several quotations from

---

1. *On Your Marks* (*Journey into Life* by Norman Warren, combined with NIV of Mark's Gospel). Published by Pocket Testament League.

it still survive in other early Christian writings, especially those that the 'father of church history', Eusebius, referred to another century later.

Papias was evidently a chummy, garrulous old man who loved name-dropping. That is understandable: he had met several people (in *his* youth and *their* old age) who had personally met Jesus or one of his first disciples. The lost five books seem to have been a wonderful jumble of gossip, anecdotes, recollections and oral traditions; tales passed on by first generation Christians (mainly Jewish, as Papias himself probably was).

One of the tales concerns the writing of this Gospel:

> Mark, who had been Peter's interpreter, wrote down care-fully, but not in order, all that he remembered of the Lord's sayings and doings. For he had not heard the Lord or been one of his followers, but later as I said, one of Peter's. Peter used to adapt his teachings to the occasion, without making a systematic arrangement of the Lord's sayings, so that Mark was quite justified in writing down some things just as he remembered them. For he had one purpose only – to leave out nothing that he heard, and to make no mis-statement about it.[2]

Papias sets this scene in Rome. The picture he draws is circumstantial and persuasive. Peter's preaching would indeed have revolved around memories of Jesus' Galilee ministry. Like any good preacher, he spoke into the immediate circumstances and into the needs of his first hearers. He was communicating a message, not composing a history – 'adapting to the occasion', as Papias says.

With infuriating imprecision Papias adds that Mark did not write until the 'departure' of the apostles Peter and Paul. Does he mean after their departure for other missions, or after their

---

2. Eusebius: *The History of the Church*, Book 2:15 p. 49; Book 3:30 p. 10, Penguin, 1989.

deaths by martyrdom? More clarity here might have given us a date, since the martyrdoms probably occurred during the 64 persecution under Nero, whereas the other missions could have been ten years earlier.[3]

Modern writers and preachers have had a splendid time speculating that Mark was in fact the anonymous young man who followed Jesus, lightly clad, when the Master led his disciples to Gethsemane, and narrowly escaped arrest by leaving his only garment in the soldiers' clutching hands as he fled (Mark 14:51-52). Why else mention this otherwise irrelevant incident, except as his own sad signature? 'I too followed half-heartedly. I too forsook him. It happened again in my later life. Yet even I am not beyond redemption, for he still called me to new beginnings as he does you, the reader' (Acts 13:4-5; 13:13; 15:36-41; Colossians 3:10; 2 Timothy 4:11). Only a guess, but one that encapsulates the central message of this book, as we shall see.

Once we have the clue, there are many hints that if the words were Mark's the voice is Peter's. There are personal recollections that were not Mark's own, but could hardly be invented. For example, there is frequent mention of a particular house in Capernaum which was Jesus' adopted home and mission-base. It was the house of Peter's mother-in-law, who was healed of a fever in the first incident where it is mentioned.[4]

---

3. The *Anti-Marcionite Prologues*, a collection of pamphlets written 160-180, states that Mark, nicknamed 'stumpfingers', wrote his gospel 'after Peter departed ... to parts of Italy'. See article by W. F. Howard in Expository Times, no. 47 (135-36), pp. 534-538.

4. Mark's references to Peter's house:
1:29-35: Mother healed, whole town gathers, Jesus leaves to pray.
  2:1-2: Paralytic healed and roof broken.
3:20-34: Jesus' worried family gather outside.
  4:10: Disciples quarrel.
  7:17: Disciples question Jesus.
  9:33: Disciples taught humility and service. For Jesus' mission head-quarters, see my *Jesus, the Man and His Message*, chapter 5.

Thousands of pilgrims visit it to this day, for it is one of the best authenticated biblical sites, supported by ancient diaries and modern archaeological research.

Consider the little personal touches, of no importance to the flow of the story except that they stand clearly in Peter's memory. Take for example the story of his own call to discipleship. He remembers that two pairs of brothers were at separate points along the seashore, but in sight of each other. Simon and Andrew were 'casting' (a technical term still in use in Galilee) as they stood in the shallows and manipulated their cast-net. James and John were preparing a different kind of net, a double dragnet or seine, on the boat deck. This required them to be slightly offshore in their craft. The second group left their father and several hired men in charge as they followed Jesus, so this was a fairly large, well organised business. There we are; Mark's pen but Peter's memory (Mark 1:16-20).

By almost common consent Mark was *the first gospel writer*. Here is our prior source in the search for 'the real Jesus', so earnestly and confusedly sought by modern scholarly critics.

Indeed this is one of the few points at which most of them agree. The arguments are complicated but fairly convincing. Let me sum them up. Most of Mark's material appears again in Matthew and half of it in Luke. Each of the other two builds upon Mark's order of events. Much of the wording is identical. Every so often, however, the other two re-shape, expand or explain Mark's account, each in his own different way. It is easy to see how they did this, but difficult to imagine the reverse process. You can see how the toothpaste got from the tube onto two different brushes, but it's hard to imagine how the brushes could have put it into the tube!

The assumption is still sometimes challenged, but I find myself convinced; here is the story as it was first told. With terse brevity, almost laconic at times (two verses for Jesus' temptation in the wilderness, and no details!), the writer seems to toss the challenge to the reader: 'These are the facts, this is how it happened – make of it what you will, but ignore it at your peril.'

If the first draft was indeed written for readers in Rome, it would be hard to imagine anything more suitable for the tough, pragmatic Roman mind.

What can we make, then, of this whole idea that Mark's Gospel is really Peter's preaching in written form? The evidence is circumstantial but convincing. Many scholars feel that the tradition is so sound that if we did not have it, we should have to improvise something very like it.

Once we have the main clue, a lot of features fall into place. There are coincidental confirmations at many points in the colourful narrative, all the more impressive because they are undesigned.

In an odd way, the most convincing argument for Mark's authorship is its unlikelihood. Why would anyone *invent* or *imagine* an apostolic writer who was not really an apostle, and could hardly have been an eyewitness?

For a time in the early church *Mark* was popular. But the book soon lost ground in comparison to *Matthew*, as Christians felt an increasing need to define and defend their faith. Mark's compressed, vivid style tells a lot of what Jesus did, but little of what he *said*, and less still of what he *meant* (so it was felt).

Augustine, around 400, could refer to Mark as a mere copier and abbreviator of Matthew. If one had the full account, why bother with the Readers Digest version?

The great theologian must have been nodding for once. Mark is indeed briefer than Matthew but that is because of the *quality and depth of his writing*. He covers less ground, but covers it more thoroughly. This becomes obvious when you compare incidents similarly related by both writers. It is Matthew who condenses, not Mark. For example, the story of the storm on the lake occupies 120 words in Mark, and only 76 in Matthew. And it is Mark who recalls (or transmits) the vivid eyewitness details. You feel wetter and more windblown in Mark's storm, more threatened by Mark's demoniac, and more pushed around in Mark's crowd – and you are *there*.[5]

Ironically, it was the critical scholars of the nineteenth century who restored the 'Second Gospel' to its rightful place. They realised that it is in fact the first Gospel. Or at least they theorized with considerable persuasiveness. Now Mark's value could be seen in all its bright glory. For he was

> '... the saint who first found grace to pen
> that Life which was the light of men'.[6]

At a time when 'the quest for the real Jesus' was at its height, here was a vital collection of clues of immense value. Like a great rocky promontory looming out of the seas and fogs of speculation and memory, here was a solid base of fact. And so early written! If Mark penned his account in 55, then Jairus' little daughter, allegedly raised from the dead in Capernaum, would still have been in her twenties (Mark 5:21-43). Unless the story were strictly true, she and dozens of doubtless garrulous relatives could have indignantly objected to the whole story as a fabrication or a ridiculous exaggeration. After all, the details were clear enough. This was no vague tale about some anonymous family in some unspecified place. Her father (named) was the synagogue ruler in a large metropolitan centre; the equivalent today would be the mayor, the chief of police and the bishop, rolled into one – of a city the equivalent of Newcastle. And if someone dismisses this as fundamental-ist overstatement (since ancient communications made such a challenge unrealistic) the polite but firm rejoinder must be 'You're wrong.' For the clear evidence is that from the earliest years Mark was universally accepted, widely known, and

---

5. Storm on the Lake (Mark 4:35-41). Notice details of Jesus 'just as he was', the furious squall, and Jesus 'in the stern sleeping' (the only covered area in a first-century Galilee fishing boat).
6. R. V. Tasker, quoted in *Mark, Evangelist & Theologian* by Ralph P Martin.

quoted throughout the empire. The challenge was there, and known to be there.

Mark calls to the reader 'Stand and deliver!' In modern parlance he puts the reader 'on the spot'. Appealing to imagination and conscience he says '*Choose*'. Very well. How does he throw down his challenge? Read on!

Chapter 5

WRITING WITH PASSION

Amidst a buzz of expectation; the curtains of a London theatre part to reveal one actor. For two hours he holds the audience spellbound as he recites the Authorised Version of Mark's Gospel from beginning to end. It happens each evening for several successive weeks; a tribute both to the actor's skill and to the gripping narrative that he handled.[1]

Mark's vigorous style makes reading a delight, and listening an adventure. Direct, active, terse, almost abrupt, it carries the reader along at a breathless pace. The sparkling sentences move in simple sequences of nouns and verbs. They are often linked by the repetitive use of the word 'and' (as the Authorised Version makes clear, but modern translations disguise). This is a deliberate device which sounds clumsy to modern ears, but in its time was very effective. The technical term for it is *parataxis*.

A favourite word of Mark's is *eutheos*, which means 'immediately'. The Authorised Version translates it rather endearingly as 'forthwith', 'straightway' or 'anon'. As a child I was puzzled by these archaic words and yet somehow knew instinctively what they implied. The writer is telling us that what Jesus had to do, he did promptly and decisively, striding into situations with life-changing imperatives.

Another habit of this enthusiastic chronicler is to use the Greek prefixes *eis* and *ek* in frequent juxtaposition. They mean

1. The actor was Alec McCowan. He records his motives and impressions in his book *Personal Mark.*

'into' and 'out of'. English translations (quite properly) obscure the repetitive use by employing a variety of words like 'entered' instead of 'went into', and 'left' instead of 'went out of'. Mark's first chapter, in one short section (verses 9-39), uses one or other of these two words seventeen times. There was, we could say, a lot of coming and going! The impression Mark wants to give us is that of Jesus constantly intervening in people's lives and never leaving them quite as he found them.

Stories with a punch-line

As we continue to look at the writer's style, we spot other clues that point to his message. He scatters the narrative with what are often called *pronouncement stories*. An incident is described with terse brevity, and ends with a succinct saying of Jesus. This 'pronouncement' not only sums up the lesson to be learned from the incident, but epitomises some truth basic to Jesus' ministry and message.

Chapter 2 provides three examples. Levi the tax-man is called to discipleship and throws a celebratory meal that shocks the respectably religious. Jesus refutes their criticism with a blunt comment that epitomises the gospel: 'It is not the healthy who need a doctor but the sick. I have not come to call the righteous but sinners.'

Two more incidents follow, leading to two more pronouncements. After an argument about religious observation, we learn that 'no-one pours new wine into old wine skins'. After an incident that raises questions over holy days, we learn that 'the Sabbath was made for man, not man for the Sabbath'.

Any reader would benefit from the exercise of reading through the book, marking the pronouncement stories and underlining the one-verse truth to which each points. Put them all together, and you have a vivid picture of the barrier-breaking Christ whose good news of God's kingdom changes people's lives at the deepest level. Here is one kind of answer to the question, 'What was Jesus like?'

Sandwich stories

Now look for another feature. The technical name is *inter-collating*. Mark writes two successive stories in such a way that they fold around each other to make what I call story sandwiches. The best-known example illustrates what I mean. Jesus receives an urgent call for help; the little daughter of Jairus the synagogue ruler is desperately ill. He immediately sets off across the town in response – but his progress (and the reader's) is interrupted by the whole story of a nameless woman with an embarrassing haemorrhage, who reaches out to touch the tassels of his prayer-shawl and is healed. Only after this does Jesus continue to Jairus' house, to find that the delay has been fatal – and raises the girl back to life. The first story wrapped around the second.[2]

Now we need not doubt that the two incidents did in fact happen in quick succession. But Mark goes out of his way to intertwine them in order to create a tension and point up a moral. He often does it more briefly, and with great effect. One of the most poignant examples is the sandwiching of Judas' betrayal of Jesus between two supper stories.[3] The first meal (at Bethany) illustrates a forgiven sinner's love for Christ. The second (in Jerusalem) shows Christ's love for sinners, in instituting the Last Supper. Between the two scenes is sandwiched the sinister figure of the betrayer, who knows nothing of either love. We need to mark sandwich stories in our margin, too!

---

2. Jairus' daughter and the woman with internal bleeding (Mark 5:21-43).
3. Two meals and a betrayal (Mark 14:1-26). The incident of Judas is sandwiched into verses 10-11. In fact, with subtlety, Mark creates several successive sandwich-stories. Judas appears on both sides of the prayer in Gethsemane (14:10, 43). Peter's denial of Jesus is hinted at before the arrest and carried out after (14:29-31, 66-72). In each case, repetitive or reminiscent wording shows the technique to be conscious and deliberate.

Faith stories

Another sharp technique of the writer is to present cameos of
faith in action – or sometimes faith failing. This is underlined
not only in the use of literal words 'have faith' and 'believe',
but in the deliberate heightening of contrast between different
attitudes. There are those who understand, but others who
merely hear. There are those who see but fail to perceive (4:10-
12).

There are the disciples who learn (however slowly) and
religious leaders who learn nothing, because their minds are
made up. As early as the end of chapter 4, the challenge comes:
'Why are you so afraid? Do you still have no faith?' (verse 40).
Only a chapter later, the challenge is the same, though the
context is different: 'Don't be afraid; just believe' (5:36). In
the very next scene we are startled to read that when Jesus re-
visited his childhood home of Nazareth, 'He could not do any
miracles there. ... And he was amazed at their lack of faith'
(6:5, 6).

As we shall see, this provides a vital clue to the writer's
whole presentation of Christ's gospel. It demands faith. Is
Mark here deliberately echoing the apostle Paul's great doctrine of saving faith? The John Mark of the biblical record had
spent as much time with Paul as with Peter.

The medium and the message

Enough has been said to show that Mark brilliantly employs
literary style in order to get across a theological message.
Swift sequences of events; vivid word pictures; deliberate
contrasts; challenges to faith and decision: here is more than
a string of well-told stories. Mark has a proclamation to make
in writing, as surely as his mentors Peter and Paul made in
preaching. I cannot trace the first reference amongst modern
Bible scholars to 'pearls on a string', but it has entered into the
language of Bible-criticism. Perhaps good old Papias started
it, with his comment that Mark did not write 'in order'. The

stories, it is often said, are linked together in a haphazard and almost muddled way. At some point, a nineteenth-century scholar used the analogy of pearls casually strung together on a cord, and the phrase has stuck.

A twentieth-century scholar, Morna Hooker, has wittily pointed out the fallacy in this idea. Only a man, she suggests, would imagine that pearls are strung together haphazardly. Any woman would have spotted at once the flaw in the analogy; pearls need to be carefully selected and graded. And gradually it has dawned on New Testament scholars that this is precisely what (each of) the evangelists have done with their material – they are making a particular theological point.[4] This is clearly true, and Mark does it as brilliantly as his fellow-writers. The medium displays the message. Mark may not record much of Jesus' teaching, but his book is pregnant with doctrine. Let me give one more example.

In on the secret
There are two alternative ways to approach the writing of a book about real or imaginary people. The author may tell the tale from the viewpoint of one character in the story (he, she or I). We, the readers, are therefore only allowed to see the thoughts of that character. We explore situations only as they happen to that one person. We stumble along with Doctor Watson seeing it only from his limited view until, at the end, Sherlock Holmes reveals all!

The second method is for the writer to stand outside and above the events. The reader is told what several people are thinking, saying and doing in different places. Agatha Christie sometimes adopted this method in her first chapter: the reader watches the characters gathering in response to the mysterious invitation, revealing their different circumstances as they come. In a certain type of detective novel, the reader may even be told the solution on the first page. The fascination then

---

4. M. Hooker, *The Message of Mark*, chapters 1 and 2, but especially p. 3.

depends on watching how the characters discover what the reader knows from the start. Will *they* spot the clues? When will the penny drop?

With great skill Mark adopts this second style. He knows how the story will finish. He explains it to the reader from the beginning (literally his first sentence). The reader knows. But the characters don't know. They stumble along, putting it together as they may. We see the bewilderment of the wonder-hungry crowds, the growing hostility of the religious establishment, and the slow, limping progress of the disciples towards faith and commitment.

So Mark lets us into the secret in his opening paragraph. This is where the good news starts (he says). And this is the faith-confession to which it leads: Jesus is the promised Christ and the Son of God. Let me invite witnesses to give their evidence. Old Testament prophets like Isaiah saw his coming; John the Baptist announced his arrival; at his baptism, God himself bore witness in the descending dove-like Spirit and affirming voice from heaven; even Satan and his minions are compelled to bear reluctant witness (read the first thirteen verses, and see if this is so).

This shared secret shapes the design of the book. Halfway through the story, the disciples have grasped it, and confess 'You are the Christ.' At the cross itself, the officer in charge realizes, 'This was the Son of God.' But the reader can know it from the start.[5]

---

5. Peter's confession of faith (Mark 8:27-30). The centurion's confession (Mark 15:37-39). Notice that the Roman soldier's cry, 'Surely this man was the Son of God', takes the reader back to the opening paragraph of the book, 'The beginning of the gospel about Jesus Christ, the Son of God'.

Chapter 6

MARK'S PORTRAIT OF JESUS

I have on my bookshelf a facsimile of the ancient Lindisfarne Gospels. This collection of the four evangelists dates back to the arrival of the first Irish missionaries in Scotland, and then on to northern England. Here they made their base on the wind-swept tidal island just south of Berwick, and, through incessant missionary journeys 'to every hilltop, wild and remote settlement' (as their chronicler says), carried the good news of a liberating Christ to the whole kingdom of Northumbria. The beautiful 'illuminated' books, ablaze with colour and symbolic art formed both their devotional tools and their evangelistic weapons. In the quiet island base the missionary-monks poured out their prayer and praise by carefully copying and illustrating the Psalms and the Gospels. In every hamlet and market square of the mainland they held aloft the beautiful pages and announced: 'God wants you to know him; here is his Word: listen to the good news of his Son.'

When these lovely volumes were produced, it had already become a Christian custom to identify the four different Gospel portraits of Christ with the four mysterious 'creatures' clustered around the throne of God in the symbolic vision of the prophet Ezekiel (chapter 1). Each had four faces; that of a man, a lion, an ox and an eagle. The image is repeated in Revelation 4:6-8.

At Lindisfarne the custom was continued with elaborately decorated frontispieces for each individual author. So Mark is pictured with the face of a lion, in the usual tradition, whilst other symbols around the page imply dynamic activity.

This is wholly appropriate; no animal is more powerful than a lion, and no other Gospel presents such a picture of dynamic intervention as Mark's. I have tried to show how the writer of this sparkling tale uses many tricks of style and description to present Jesus to the reader. Now here is the heart of the question: What is he actually *telling* us about 'the real Jesus'? If each evangelist paints a different word-portrait of Christ, what are the lineaments of his face in Mark's picture?

To discover that, we need to grasp the overall shape and structure of the book. There is nothing casual or thrown together about it. No pearls strung together haphazardly!

How Peter preached
We find the plan of the book (I want to suggest) in a surprising place. I can still recall the thrill with which I first noticed it, and naïvely felt it to be my own personal discovery. According to tradition Mark was Peter's assistant in Rome, reporting and summarizing his preaching. But we already know how that same Peter spoke the message to Romans when he so reluctantly shed his religious and racial prejudices in order to take it to a military household in Caesarea, on the coast of Palestine. The idea offended him as a strictly orthodox Jew who embraced the purity laws, but God left him no option. An odd vision, a divine voice and some unexpected visitors all pressed him into preaching his first non-Jewish sermon.

We find the story in Acts 10. The sermon-outline appears as verses 34-43. Let me pick out the main features, and show how *Mark's Gospel follows exactly the same pattern*.

'The good news of peace through Jesus Christ' (Acts 10:36). (Mark begins 'the good news about Jesus Christ'.)

'Beginning in Galilee after the baptism that John preached' (10:37). (Mark introduces John the Baptizer, and then sends Jesus to Galilee.)

'How God anointed Jesus of Nazareth with the Holy Spirit and power' (10:38). (Mark describes exactly that.)

'And how he went around doing good and healing all who were under the power of the devil' (10:38). (Mark spends the first eight chapters describing a thrilling series of healings and exorcisms.)

'We are witnesses of everything he did in the country of the Jews and in Jerusalem' (10:39). (From chapter 9 Mark ends the Galilee ministry and builds up the tension as Jesus leads his disciples south through Judaea to confrontation in Jerusalem – a basic theme of the book, as I have demonstrated.)

'They killed him by hanging him on a tree, but God raised him on the third day' (10:39-40). (Mark 15 and 16 are filled with this, in stark unvarnished detail.)

So Peter's sermon and Mark's scroll both end with a commission to announce forgiveness and salvation to all who believe.

The resemblance is remarkable, and cannot be coincidental. Here is the redeeming message as Peter (and therefore Mark) sees it. The good news is the story of God's saving action in his Son Jesus. Anointed by the Spirit, he sweeps into action, setting Galilee alight with works of deliverance and mercy. But after the initial excitement there is confusion and disappointment.

What kind of Messiah is this? Certainly not the kind that was expected by the masses! He comes to seek, serve and save, rather than threaten, display and conquer. He avoids publicity whenever possible. He discourages excitement and wild claims. He makes no effort to placate his opponents or defuse their criticisms. Even his closest followers are puzzled, and very slow to learn.

Then he walks deliberately to his death, warning that it cannot be avoided and is willingly endured. That death, he teaches, will pay a ransom, seal a covenant and open the way to God (10:45;14:24). There is liberation in the cross, but not from political powers or military foes. And, at the end, when the tomb is found empty, he still 'goes before' those who trust and follow (16:7).

So Jesus himself is his gospel! That preliminary statement was Mark's first word, and it is his last. God's Son does not merely announce God's kingdom: he personifies it.

The message focused

Finally, we must ask a related question. What picture does Mark present of the Christian life that flows from confidence in Jesus? It is essentially a life that reflects the faith, obedience, servanthood and victory-through-suffering of the Son of God.

First, it is an *invitation to faith in God*. The challenge to 'believe' and to 'have faith' features in story after story; a constant refrain on the lips of Jesus as we have seen. It is first and foremost a faith in God rather than in Jesus. Not that one contradicts the other, of course. The God who beckons us to believe in him is no abstract concept required by reason or taught by tradition. He is the God who uniquely declares his powerful rule and saving love *in Jesus*. That is why, to Mark's mind, the good news of Jesus is the good news of the kingdom, which is the good news of God (1:1, 15).

What can we know of this God in whom Jesus calls us to believe? He is sovereign; in charge of events, even when it may seem that events are out of anyone's control. Nothing happens, either for good or ill, outside God's control. It is no coincidence that the first letter to be written by an apostle describes Christian conversion in exactly the same terms as this first narrative to be written by an apostle's friend. 'You turned to God from idols to serve the living and true God, and to wait for his Son from heaven ... Jesus who rescues us from the coming wrath' (1 Thessalonians 1:9-10). Here indeed is good news for people disillusioned with their dead deities (whether those of the first century, or ours of the twentieth, like secularism, Marxism, monetarism, materialism or the beckoning sirens of self and personal gratification). There is a living God, made known in Jesus, who welcomes us to living faith in him.

Second, it is *a call to follow Jesus.* For Mark, Jesus is the unique example of what it means to have total faith in God and to give total obedience to God. The life of faith is the life we see Jesus living. This is why his healing miracles and exorcisms must not be seen as mere examples of 'faith healing' or expositions of the 'faith formula'. Jesus' actions spring from total confidence in God's wise, good and gracious purposes wherever they might lead. For him, they led to service for others, and then to the cross and resurrection. For us they will lead to various kinds of service and cross-carrying, but through them to life indeed, shared with God.

This is why the lengthy climax of Mark's story (that long journey from Caesarea Philippi to Calvary) is so full of the theme of *following.* We constantly read of Jesus 'going ahead' or 'leading the way' and his disciples as 'following on the way' (10:32). There is a deliberate double meaning in Mark's choice of words. The Master was walking a physical highway. The disciples literally followed a few steps behind, whispering to each other their perplexities, doubts, fears and even quarrels as they found the purpose and direction so puzzling. At the end of each day's journey he confronted those whispers with an explanation and sometimes a rebuke (4:10-12; 10:14-15). But in a much more profound sense, he was walking *a pathway of obedience to God,* whilst they limped behind, slowly learning what it really meant to 'follow'.

Two consecutive scenes of great poignancy make that particularly clear. They are (still) 'on their way up to Jerusalem'. Something about the Master's grim expression as he faces the imminent prospect of great suffering fills the disciples with foreboding, and they hang back astonished whilst the

wider group of followers lingers even further back 'following,
afraid'. Jesus takes them aside and spells out again what awaits
him: betrayal, mockery, flogging and death – then resurrection. This is the path that must be pursued. Their response is
bizarre in its gross misunderstanding. Two of them ask if they
can have the honour of sitting at his right and left hand in glory.
The others indignantly join in the place-pushing. They still
have no idea what 'following' really means. Jesus then draws
his famous word-picture of the kingdom-values in which the
way up is down; the path to leadership is lowly service: 'For
even the Son of Man did not come to be served, but to serve,
and to give his life as a ransom for many' (10:45).

Immediately afterwards (in Mark's deliberate and subtle
sandwiching of events) comes that perennially fresh story of
'Blind Bartimaeus'. Evangelists and Sunday school teachers
have used it a thousand times to illustrate what it means to meet
Christ and to follow him. Their instinct is sound even when
they are not aware of how skilfully Mark employs the Greek
language to point up the lesson. Here are all the double-
meanings of physical and spiritual significance. The blind
man (a symbol of moral and spiritual confusion) sits beside the
highway (for he cannot walk along it). Hearing of Jesus
passing by, he shouts in dawning faith: 'Jesus, Son of David,
have mercy on me.' People do their best to discourage him (as
they often will) but he persists. Jesus stops and calls him,
deliberately and personally. 'Throwing his cloak aside' (anything that might catch around his legs and hinder his progress)
he comes eagerly to Jesus. Spelling out his need ('I want to
see') he receives the word of new life, ('your faith has healed
you'). What is the result? *Immediately* (that word *eutheos*,
used so often of Jesus' own swift response to God's call and
mankind's need) he received his sight and *followed Jesus
along the road* (that same familiar phrase with its double
meaning: 10:46-52).

Nor is that all. In the final scene at the empty tomb,

astonished women are told to pass on to the disciples the simple message that the Risen Christ 'is going ahead of you (same phrase again) into Galilee'. Always they must follow (16:6-7). The good news is that a way has been opened for us to follow, freed from the clinging bonds of sin, fear, tradition and self-centredness.

Thirdly, the gospel *is an uplifting of the cross*. That in two senses. What Jesus did uniquely on the cross was to pay a ransom for our freedom, to open the way to forgiveness of sins, and to break the power of those forces that enslave us. But also by going so willingly to the cross in obedience to God's call and mankind's need, he opens up a pattern of servant-living for his liberated people to follow.[1] That is good news: the possibility of freedom from the downward pull of selfishness, self-exaltation and self-indulgence.

Today's gospel: Is it Christ's?
All of this leaves us with disturbing questions. Evangelical Christians today glory in the good news, and feel themselves called to its clear and pressing proclamation. The very words *evangelist* and *evangelical* are anglicisms of those great words of Jesus, variously translated 'gospel' and 'good news'. Then are we presenting it in a way consistent with his own terms? Such questions may compel us to think again about our need-centred, satisfaction-based invitations to 'believe'. Are they really calls for commitment to a mighty, sovereign God – or are they invitations to have faith in faith, as a means to get what we want and think we need? Do we promote a Jesus who improves our self-image and makes us feel better, or a biblical Christ who strides into our lives, setting us free to give and serve as we follow him?

---

1. For example, the turning point of the story (Mark 8:27-38). Note: 'the Son of Man must suffer ... if anyone would come after me, he must ... take up his cross'. See also 9:31 and 10:33-34.

Matthew

Chapter 7

MATTHEW – THE CHURCH HANDBOOK

If approaching Mark is like opening a newspaper, turning to Matthew is more like scanning a church membership manual. Here, above all else, is the good news taught. Modern studies of this Gospel underline that idea, with titles like 'Matthew, the Teacher's Gospel'.[1] Some even suggest that the author was a converted rabbi, and thus maintain that he could not at the same time be a converted tax collector, as the character of that name was said to be!

It may sound odd to describe any New Testament writer as a Christian scribe, when that class of gentlemen gets such a bad press in the story of Jesus (and is indeed regarded as far more villainous than the unpopular tax-man). Matthew's book in particular records Jesus' devastating denunciations of Jewish teachers and scribes.

However, that is only part of the picture. His book also records Jesus' word-cameo of 'every teacher of the law who has been instructed about the kingdom', comparing them with a delighted householder exploring some abandoned room and discovering 'treasures new and old' (13:52). Is this little quote another 'autograph' quietly slipped in, like Mark's reference to the under-dressed youth at midnight?

Certainly the picture of kingdom treasures new and old exactly describes this remarkable book, for so long referred to as 'the First Gospel' because it was the early church's foundation teaching handbook. *Evangelical Instruction* just about sums it up.

---

1. e.g. Paul Minear, *Matthew, the Teacher's Gospel*.

Some commentators go further. A well-known feature of the book is the presence of its five blocks of Jesus' teaching, separated but linked by blocks of anecdotes and incidents. Could they be five teaching manuals, already in use in the early church, and incorporated into Matthew's writing? Or, for that matter, written by him in the first place and then combined into one gospel scroll?

I like the idea: it appeals to my own instinct for teaching allied to evangelism, and my experience of how it works. In fact I have my own mental labels for the imagined booklets:

A handbook of Christian Ethics: chapters 5-7
A handbook for Itinerant Evangelists: chapter 10
A handbook of Kingdom Teaching: chapter 13
A handbook for Church Members: chapter 18
A handbook of Prophetic Signs: chapters 24-25

It all reminds me of the various Membership Classes, Foundation Courses, Baptismal Instructions and the like, so successfully used by those very churches that are making most impact today.

The prize for popularity

Without doubt Matthew's Gospel was the most widely used volume in the church's accumulating collection that eventually became the New Testament. All of the 'early fathers' of the first and second centuries either directly quoted Matthew, or referred constantly to him. Clement of Rome, Ignatius of Antioch, Jerome of Jerusalem, Justin the great apologist to the Jews – all regarded Matthew's Gospel as their foundation source for the teaching of Jesus. In one book alone, his *Dialogue*, Justin has forty-two references. The *Didache*, a booklet almost certainly written in the lifetime of some of the apostles, has its full title 'The Teaching of the Twelve Apostles'. The title deliberately echoes Matthew's record of Jesus' missionary commission, and its pages are full of Matthean quotes or references.

I think it would be fair to say that the first-century church's climate of opinion and practice was created by this narrative of Matthew's.[2] As R.T. France says, it established itself as the gospel *par excellence*; the book to read for an authoritative account of the words and deeds of Jesus. The marks of a skilled teacher are on every page. The systematic alternating of Jesus' words and deeds (in great blocks of teaching followed by action stories that illustrate the truth being taught), creates a completely different atmosphere from that of Mark. This is less vivid perhaps, but more conducive to thought and discussion. If Mark grips the imagination and appeals to the emotion, then Matthew addresses the mind and beckons to the will.

Who wrote it?

The early church that used the book so widely, unanimously agrees that it was written by the member of the apostolic band variously called Matthew and Levi.[3] Origen tells us, for example, that the author was Matthew, once a tax collector but later an apostle of Jesus Christ who published it for those who had come to the Christian faith from Judaism, and that it was composed in Hebrew letters.[4]

He may have got this from the garrulous Papias whose gossip column we have already consulted, but not necessarily so. Papias' reference was short and succinct on this occasion:

---

2. Early opinions of Matthew's Gospel: R. T. France gives a fascinating summary in *Matthew – Evangelist and Teacher*, pp. 13-27.

3. Matthew the apostle in the New Testament: Matthew 9:9 and 10:3 compared to Mark 2:14 and Luke 5:27 (see the context, in each case). Scholars have found signs of 'special interest in financial matters' in several parts of the book, which might indicate a profession of local government officer (Matthew 17:24-27; 18:23-25; 20:1-16; 28:11-15)!

4. Origen's reference to Matthew in a commentary on that book which briefly described the origins of all four Gospels, comes to us via Eusebius, 6:25:3-6 (p. 201 of the translation by Williamson).

'Matthew compiled the *Sayings* in the Aramaic language, and everyone translated them as well as he could.'[5]

Although modern scholars dislike the idea, there is much in its favour, and nothing improbable about it. A local government official would be a good candidate for secretary and recorder of the little band of disciples. Someone skilled in tachygraphy, an early form of shorthand (as a tax collector would undoubtedly be) was well placed to record the words of Jesus as they were spoken. There is some evidence that travelling rabbis employed both note-takers and memorisers to preserve and promulgate their message. There is something attractive in the thought of the new convert bringing a crooked skill from his old pursuit (tax collectors were dishonest almost by definition) and committing it to the new task of recording and disseminating the truth.

Several times I have re-told the story to youth-groups (suitably embellished with the desk crashing over as the startled clerk rushes out of the little tax-booth to follow the call). Hearers respond to that same call, and offer whatever talents they possess, cleansed and re-directed, to the service of Christ. I think, for example, of a secular-minded trainee social worker who turned to become a Salvation Army Officer.

Unlikely allies
Matthew-Levi responded by throwing a party for his erstwhile associates (a dubious crew in the eyes of the respectable) and inviting them to meet Jesus (9:9-13). This in itself was highly significant: a declaration of the nature of that new community into which Christ was calling people.[6]

If his conversion was surprising, his inclusion in the apostolic team was sensational. A tax collector was widely regarded as a tool of Rome, a collaborator with God's enemies

---

5. Papias' reference to Matthew: Book 3:39 (p. 105 of the translation by Williamson).
6. The reconciled community: see my *Jesus, the Man and His Message*, chapter 3, 'The Man Who Broke Barriers'.

and his country's conquerors. Yet in that same group of disciples was one Simon the Zealot, otherwise known as the Patriot.[7] The Zealot party was a politico-religious group of revolutionaries violently opposed to the Roman occupation. To Zealots, the only good Roman was a dead one, and the same applied to collaborators. Depending on the observer's point of view, they were regarded as freedom-fighters, urban guerrilla terrorists, brigands, or religious extremists. Comparison with today's PLO, Hezb'ollah, Ulster paramilitaries or the IRA would not be too fanciful. For Simon and Levi to work together was an astonishing example of reconciliation.

As I've suggested, some scholars have questioned whether Matthew the publican, an outcast from synagogue life, could possibly be Matthew the skilled teacher with his Jewish-oriented understanding and his love of the Hebrew scriptures. But his alternative name Levi at least suggests a religious background from which he had lapsed. In any case, conversion can effect radical change. I know a trainrobber who became an evangelist, and a tramp who became a skilled theologian preparing others for the ministry. Nothing is impossible or unlikely in Christ's kingdom!

The town by the sea

Matthew lived and worked in Capernaum; that too is significant. Sprawling beside the north western shore of Galilee lake, 'Nahum's town' (as the name means) dominated the major highways of the province. An archaeologist standing with me in today's excavated and partly restored town estimated that as many as eleven distinct taxes would be chargeable there (road tax, bridge tax, harbour tax, fish tax, grain tax, and so on). Yet the province was also the very heart of the Zealot movement. Plots, insurrections, betrayals, internal feuds, fanaticism, seething subterranean anger – all were commonplace here. It was quite unlike the sentimental images encouraged

---

7. Simon the Zealot, and the apostolic team (Matthew 10:1-4).

by some writers of children's story-bibles, who seem to think that because Jesus sometimes talked about flowers, everyone spent their time picking them or playing amongst them. The physical climate, the religious climate and the political climate were equally sultry and threatening.

This is no digression. It brings me to the heart of Matthew's message. He introduces Jesus' ministry in unforgettable words, typically drawn from ancient prophecy. Jesus 'returned to Galilee. Leaving Nazareth, he went and lived in Capernaum, which was by the lake in the area of Zebulon and Naphtali – to fulfil what was said through the prophet Isaiah:

' "Land of Zebulon and land of Naphtali,
      the way to the sea, along the Jordan,
      Galilee of the Gentiles –
the people living in darkness
      have seen a great light
on those living in the land of the shadow of death
      a light has dawned."

'From that time Jesus began to preach, "Repent, for the kingdom of heaven is near" ' (4:12-17).

The light dawns
Some of us once climbed a hill above the lake before sunrise. We watched the gloom of the mountain and valleys slowly give way to the first tremulous hints of dawn. The light crept across the distant sky in pearl and pink and pale orange, until the sun leapt over the horizon, scattering the pewter waters of the lake with ripples of silver and then gold. The light had come – as it did to that dark, disturbed and desperate society of Matthew's, constantly agitated by rumour and uprising which repeatedly exploded in riot and then faded away in pain and disillusionment.

The words of Jesus must have met with rapturous excite-

ment at first. He gathered crowds. He worked wonders. He
spoke with a new authority. He invoked the magic word
'Kingdom'. Surely – this time – ?

But disappointment quickly followed. The Kingdom Manifesto (so carefully recorded in Matthew, in what we now call
the Sermon on the Mount) portrayed priorities that made no
sense of their violent dreams, and exploded their Messianic
hopes.

> Blessed are the poor in spirit.
> The meek will inherit the earth.
> Show mercy.
> Make peace.
> Don't judge.

What was all this about forgiving enemies, walking the second
mile and turning the other cheek? What kind of kingdom was
this? What kind indeed? Matthew tells us. One in which God
reigns in human hearts, repentance is shown by changed
direction, and God's forgiving fatherhood is welcomed with
humble joy. Not really what Galilee wanted to hear!

This is Matthew's story: the king who came to reign, but
whose rule is like no other's.

Outline of the story
This key-thought of kingship provides a useful outline for the
whole book. Here is my own suggestion of the way in which
it can be read.

Prologue: *The Man born to be King* (chapters 1-2).
A genealogy proclaims him, and 'wise men' seek him.

Part One: *The Good News of the kingdom* (chapters 3-9).
Jesus is anointed and acknowledged at his baptism. He announces his 'manifesto' in the Sermon on the Mount. His

deeds illumine his words in a series of interventions in people's lives, displaying authority over disease, distance, demons and despair (a rich vein here for preachers!).

Part Two: *Ambassadors of the kingdom* (chapters 10-12). Jesus sends out his evangelists, armed only with compassion and commitment.

Part Three: *The Secrets of the kingdom* (chapters 13-16). Having explained the true meaning of his rule in a series of brilliant but enigmatic parables, Jesus ever more openly offers himself as the heart of his message. At the turning point of the book (16:13-28) he challenges crowds and disciples alike with the question of his own identity.

Part Four: *The Progress of the King* (chapters 17-20). Owned by words from God when in transfigured glory, he continues to teach and heal, but with two increased emphases: he must suffer, and his followers are called to a changed life.

Part Five: *The Passion of the King* (chapters 21-27). Jesus enters Jerusalem with obvious Messianic symbolism, and for a dramatic week confronts the religious leaders with their false values. Infuriated, they arrest him and have him crucified. The Roman power puts a charge above his head: THIS IS JESUS, THE KING OF THE JEWS.

Epilogue: *The Man with Authority* (chapter 28). Christ rises from the dead. He commissions his followers to teach and convert the nations with his authority. The direction of the Prologue is reversed: then the Gentiles came seeking him; now his ambassadors go seeking the Gentiles.

This, I suggest, offers a simple and memorable outline. Each section has its easily-spotted core-text. Thus:

Prologue 'Where is the one who has been born king of the Jews?' (2:2)

Part 1 'Theirs is the kingdom of heaven' (5:3).

Part 2 'Preach this message – the kingdom of heaven is near' (10:7).

Part 3 'The knowledge of the secrets of the kingdom has been given to you' (13:11).

Part 4 (God says) 'This is my Son. Listen to him' (17:5).

Part 5 'See, your king comes to you' (21:5).

Epilogue 'All authority ... has been given to me ... go and make disciples' (28:19-20).

There is a great theme: Christ's Kingship. We now see how Matthew will present it with passion and persuasiveness.

Chapter 8

THE MAN BORN TO BE KING

The officials at Tel Aviv airport were embarrassed. The traveller whom they questioned was a Jewish Christian. He was known to have been answering enquiries (there was nothing clandestine about it) from Israeli conscript soldiers who were considering becoming followers of Jesus of Nazareth. The problem for the authorities was this: how would Hebrew Christian soldiers treat hostile Arabs next time there was a confrontation? There were, after all, some very difficult sections in the Sermon on the Mount about loving your enemies!

This bizarre incident in the experience of an acquaintance of mine illustrates how topical, how searching and potentially explosive is Matthew's Gospel in today's world. The Middle East Peace Process is a crucial element in world affairs as the century draws towards its close. In an age of space-flight, nuclear energy and electronic communication highways a little scroll addressed to Hebrew Christians nineteen centuries ago is pointedly and painfully relevant.

If its contents are explosive, its style is dynamic and its matter gripping. I have already compared Matthew's work to a teaching manual, but that certainly does not imply academic dryness. It would be equally fair to compare it with a gripping stage-drama that draws excited crowds. 'Dramatic narrative' is a phrase often used to describe it.

I can still recall the stir created during the Second World War by Dorothy Sayers' radio play-cycle, *The Man Born to be King*. It created a sensation (and a certain amount of pious scandal) by portraying the disciples with Cornish or Cockney accents, and by presenting the story of Jesus in the real situation of his time, rather than in the stained-glass and soupy voice situations of professional religion. (One listener complained at Herod's brusque command to one of his courtiers to 'shut your mouth'. The listener found it impossible to believe that 'someone associated with our Lord' would use such a coarse expression!)[1]

My point is this: Dorothy Sayers knew her job. For the interplay of character and collision, of speech and action which make a good play what it is, she went to Matthew for her model. Her very title comes from the words of the Christmas Magi: 'Where is the one who has been born King of the Jews?' (Matthew 2:1-2). The whole theme of kingship, the material of the teaching, the dialogue, and the mounting tension of the plays, are all drawn from Matthew's magnificent and memorable narrative.

Perhaps Matthew appeals especially to me because I am by vocation a preacher, a teacher and a writer – and also have a 'strong weakness' for good drama! First let me show you how skilfully he deploys word and phrase, tensions and contrasts, to achieve his end. Then we can examine what it is he tells us about Jesus the King.

Old story, new style
Matthew re-tells Mark's story: the pattern of events is the same, but he cannot be accused of repetition. Everything he touches he makes his own. Here is the familiar outline again: baptism in Jordan, ministry of healing in Galilee, crisis of identity ('Who do you say I am?') and journey to Jerusalem for conflict, suffering, death and resurrection. But Matthew handles it his own way. He reveals the single-minded purpose of the teacher rather than the eager eloquence of the raconteur.

---

1. *The Man Born to be King,* a radio play-cycle by Dorothy L. Sayers, first broadcast by the BBC in 1940, and published as a book in 1943.

He focuses in to the vital core of each event, resisting the lure of vivid detail to concentrate on the heart of its meaning.

Indeed, this is one of the 'problems' pinpointed by modern critics, who prefer any authorship to that traditionally accepted. How is it, they ask, that Mark who was not an eyewitness wrote as if he was, whilst Matthew who was wrote as if he was not? The first question, we have seen, has a ready answer; Mark was recording Peter's memories. The second question is easily answered too; Matthew wanted above all to *teach*. Whilst Mark seeks an emotional and imaginative impact, Matthew targets mind and memory. It is rather like the difference between a modern 'seekers course' and an older catechism class!

Nonetheless, Matthew knows how to create atmosphere. The book, though written in Greek, has a pervasive Hebrew feel about it, created by a careful choice of word and phrase.

For example, several Semitic words are simply transliterated into the Greek (and some straight through to our English Bibles). One instance is *Raca* (literally, 'damned fool', an expletive forbidden by Jesus, 5:22).

The writer has many other subtle tricks. He employs the occasional archaic and quaintly religious phrase, like 'they rejoiced with exceeding great joy' (2:10, AV), and 'He stretched forth his hand' (8:3, AV) as well as the frequent 'and behold'. The effect is much like that created by reading from the 1662 Prayer Book.

These simple devices are effective aids to memory, either in learning or liturgical worship. That is why, to this day, it is Matthew's version of the Lord's Prayer and the Beatitudes, rather than Luke's, that is commonly used in public worship. But these devices also subtly create 'atmosphere'.[2]

In similar vein, Jesus' teaching is often introduced with the quaint phrase, 'He answered and said'. Our reporter wants us

---

2. Some modern scholars have argued that Matthew draws on an early church lectionary and liturgy. It is surely more likely in reverse: that set readings and prayers drew on this Gospel for inspiration.

to pause reverently before we read words of awesome impact. There are five references to 'weeping and gnashing of teeth' (8:12; 13:42, 50; 22:13; 24:51; 25:30 AV), which have the same effect. Frequent, too, are balanced poetical phrases, often described as Hebrew parallelisms. 'Many are called, but few are chosen.' 'Wise as serpents, but harmless as doves.' Another teaching device, still popular with modern preachers, is the three-point statement or command, 'Ask, seek and knock' (10:16, AV); 'Come, take and learn' (7:7 and 11:28). I have used both of these brisk commands with more than one restless youth club during the obligatory epilogue – and could name some of those who have responded with life-changing decision.

Master of communication
Of course these last examples are not actually Matthew's words but Christ's (if we take the writer seriously, as I do). The disciple delighted to recall and record the skill of his mentor, and to copy it himself.[3] Here is the master of words at work; he who is rightly called the very *Logos* or self-communication of God, as John will say (John 1:1-14).

Formula quotations
Matthew has other verbal devices too. He often interrupts his own story with a formula like, 'So was fulfilled what was said by the prophets' (then refers back to some Old Testament incident or promise).[4] Is he referring to some collection of proof texts or 'testimonies' widely used in the early church in its debates with Jewish teachers? Such collections were certainly employed by the second century. Or is he simply

---

3. For an examination in detail of Jesus' skill with words. See my *Jesus, the Man and His Message*, pp.29-39.
4. Matthew's 'formula quotations': 1:22 (quoting Isaiah); 2:4-5 (quoting Micah); 2:14-15 (referring to Hosea); 2:23 (invoking 'the prophets'); 4:14, 8:17, 12:17 (all quoting Isaiah); 13:35 (the Psalmist); 21:4-5 (Zechariah); 26:56 (the prophets) and 27:9 (Jeremiah).

recalling his Saviour's own use of biblical 'typology' and copying that habit, exploring its possibilities with reverent delight? Whatever the motive, its consequence is clear enough: the reader is repeatedly recalled to the great notion that nothing was happening by accident. God's ages-long design was being worked out in and through his Son, Jesus.

Another repeated phrase which may well serve to provide an outline to the whole book, is first found at the end of the Sermon on the Mount: 'When Jesus had finished saying these things' (7:28). The words appear again after each of the great 'teaching blocks' to which I've already referred.[5] They serve as bridges between the teaching and the actions that follow. There is nothing casual about this: put the two together and you see how the teaching in no way interrupts the dramatic flow of the story, but adds depth and urgency to it. The skilful interweaving of word and deed carries the plot forward and heightens its mounting climax of kingdom offered, rejected yet achieved. That observation brings me back to my suggestion of 'drama' in Matthew. The long verbal discourses act very much as the soliloquies or speeches of Shakespeare's plays.

Now what is all this leading to? What is it that Matthew wants to tell us about Jesus, using all these skills of teacher, poet and dramatist? The answer is not hard to find. *Jesus is God's promised Messiah King.* He came to fulfil the ancient promises. He is the focus of all history.

I once had a long conversation with a young Jew as we stood near the Garden Tomb in Jerusalem. He told me how his search for meaning had taken him from life in London's East End to Israeli citizenship in the Holy City. He described how he explored and rejected in turn, Buddhism ('shapeless'),

---

5. Matthew's 'teaching formulae': 7:28; 11:1; 13:53; 19:1; 26:1. Intriguingly, each is followed by a change of geographical location as the next incidents unfold. The five sections may be designed to remind Jewish readers of the five books of Moses, especially when the first is followed by Jesus descending from a mountain!

Atheism ('pointless'), Zionism ('disillusioning'), and Orthodox Jewish religion ('legalistic and harsh'). He began at last,
and in some despair, to explore the ancient hope of a coming
Messiah, cherished by his own people for centuries.

'As I explored the promises this thought came powerfully
to me: What more could Messiah be, than Jesus of Nazareth
is?' So he told me. Brought at last to certainty, he was baptised
a believer in Jesus.

A story like that, multiplied a thousand times, lies behind
Matthew's Gospel. Jesus of Nazareth is presented as King of
the Jews, promised Messiah, yet Saviour of all mankind.
Matthew would have thoroughly approved of Paul's words to
the Romans, about 'the gospel (God) promised beforehand
through his prophets in the Holy Scriptures regarding his Son
... a descendant of David ... a gospel directed ... first to the Jew,
then to the Gentile'.[6]

It reminded me of my own first experience of introducing
a Jew to Jesus, years earlier in Sunderland, England. Pressing
questions about faith and meaning came from a woman whose
interest was aroused. We read together Isaiah 53 from 'her'
Bible, and Matthew 27 from 'mine'. The woman was convinced, and yielded her life to Jesus.

Christ – focus and fulfilment

Here is Matthew's central assertion. In Jesus of Nazareth are
fulfilled all God's pledges and purposes. First lived out
partially in his ancient people Israel, they were then expressed
perfectly in 'Israel's hope and consolation', her Messiah and
King. Matthew would have thoroughly approved of the carol
which, addressing Bethlehem on the first Christmas Eve, says
'The hopes and fears of all the years, are met in thee tonight'.

---

6. Romans 1:1-7. The whole passage remarkably reflects not only
Matthew's basic theme, but his closing commission to world evangelism. There is every reason to suppose that Matthew would have been
familiar with Paul's letter, which of course was written earlier.

The writer makes this clear in two ways. First, he allows Jesus to speak for himself, in powerful word and confirming deed. Then he builds his own comments and dramatic structures around that revelation, in the ways we have already examined.

How Jesus saw himself

Do not think that I have come to abolish the Law or the Prophets; I have not come to abolish them but to fulfil them (5:17).

So Jesus spelled it out, early in his formal preaching. Even earlier, his warning, 'Repent for the kingdom of heaven is near', had laid the foundation. What was long promised and longed for was now on the door-step – his coming was the coming of the kingdom. We could say that the whole, crucial difference between Jesus and the Jewish teachers who preceded him, was in a *change of tense*. They said, 'The kingdom will come.' He said, 'It is here.' The kingdom is here, for the King has come; that is the good news of God's rule.

Jesus often compared himself with those who had preceded him. With what appears to be a startling absence of modesty he described himself as greater than Jonah, Solomon and Elijah.

He quoted Moses, founding father of the faith, only to amend and deepen his teaching (5:21, 27). He used language that implied a personal and unique insight to God's purposes, with his frequent 'I say unto you'. In one pregnant chapter we have him describing himself as greater than the Sabbath regulations, the temple organisation, the Davidic kingship, the prophetic ministry, and the Solomonic glory – a gold mine for preachers who wish to fulfil their most glorious calling, which is not to beguile audiences with anecdotes but to challenge and thrill them with the wonder of God's Son (see 12:5, 8, 40, 42).

To get some idea of how this must have sounded to the first hearers, imagine someone in Britain who compares himself favourably with Arthur of the Britons, Alfred the Great, Robert the Bruce, Augustine of Canterbury, John Knox, Robin Hood, the Magna Carta and the British Constitution!

Jesus favourite title was 'the Son of Man'. So we must assume, if we judge by the number of times Matthew reports his use of it. Remember the solemn scene at his mock trial, so carefully placed at the climax of that trial and indeed as the reason for his condemnation to death. False and contradictory 'witnesses' have been produced against him and failed to carry conviction. The prisoner has, as he was entitled, declined to offer any defence. But if God himself were to be invoked under oath, then he must answer.

> The high priest said to him, 'I charge you under oath by the living God: Tell us if you are the Christ, the Son of God.'
>
> 'Yes, it is as you say,' Jesus replied. 'But I say to all of you: In the future you will see the *Son of Man* sitting at the right hand of the Mighty One and coming on the clouds of heaven.'
>
> Then the high priest tore his clothes and said, 'He has spoken blasphemy!' ... 'He is worthy of death,' they answered (26:62-66, emphasis mine).

Everyone present knew what Jesus meant. He was quoting the mysterious, majestic vision granted to the prophet Daniel – one which particularly excited and inflamed Pharisees, Zealots and Dead Sea Sectarians alike, with its hope of supernatural intervention through a divine-human figure who would be given an everlasting kingdom. The pagan nations are pictured behaving (typically) like wild beasts. Then, in contrast, a figure not beast-like but human takes their place:

> There before me was one like a son of man, coming with the clouds of heaven. He approached the Ancient of Days and was led into his presence. He was given authority, glory and sovereign power .... His dominion is an everlasting dominion that will not pass away, and his kingdom is one that will never be destroyed (Daniel 7:13-14).

Compare the prisoner's confession and the seer's vision. Son of man – clouds of heaven – presence of God: they are the same. Jesus is saying 'I am that one.' No wonder it created a sensation!

A well-known modern Jewish theologian in Jerusalem said thoughtfully to a Christian scholar, who in turn told me: 'I've come to believe that Jesus of Nazareth is the Son of Man pictured in Daniel's vision. Whether I can also accept the extra-biblical Latin and Greek titles of Christianity's great creeds, I'm not yet sure.'

Nor did this staggering statement made by Jesus come 'out of the blue' without warning or preparation. It was his favourite self-chosen title. Sometimes, admittedly, he seems to have used 'Son of man' to emphasize his genuine humanity (he is Lord of the Sabbath; made for mankind's benefit; he was homeless in his itinerant ministry; he was destined to suffer; betrayed by a false friend; busy rescuing the lost; coming to serve rather than be served).[7] Matthew, Mark and Luke equally emphasize all this. But in Matthew's own specially selected memories there is a stronger strand that echoes Daniel again and again.

There is much of clouds, heaven, coming in glory, kingdoms, angels and judgment. There are warnings of the *parousia* (the royal visit). The Son of Man will sit on his throne and judge the nations gathered before him. There will be signs in the sky at his coming. Here is the breaking in of supernatural power, the language of apocalyptic as the scholars call it.[8]

The picture is not always uniform, and Christians need to be cautious in their interpretation. Is he speaking of his first

---

7. The 'human' Son of Man, associated with God's offer of love and truth: 12:8; 13:37; 16:13; 17:9 for some examples. (Sometimes the phrase on Jesus' lips seems to mean simply 'I, as I am seen and heard by you', as in his question, 'Who do people say the Son of Man is?' (16:13) which means 'Who do people say I am?')

8. The 'divine' Son of Man; associated with judgment, glory and power: 10:23; 13:41; 16:28; 19:28; 25:31-33.

coming or his future return? Of the victory of the cross and empty tomb, or a future universal kingdom? Of the worldwide spread of the gospel or the destruction of Jerusalem's temple and the start of a new age? Of God's daily judgments, or a final Day of Reckoning? Probably all of these, in various combinations. For the basic purpose of apocalyptic is not to satisfy our curiosity, nor to encourage date-setting speculation, but to equip us to be ready, alert, faithful and obedient in *any time of God's special action* – and to recognise that his Christ-Son is crucial to all his plans.[9]

---

9. Apocalyptic hopes: see my *Jesus, The Man and His Message*, chapter 7, 'The man who glimpsed the future'.

Chapter 9

MATTHEW'S LAST GREAT ACT

I continue to suggest that Matthew's scroll can be seen as a drama of Kingship. To show in full detail how powerfully he portrays the great truth of Jesus the Fulfilment-King would require a hundred pages. Let me take, by way of example, the final great Act in the drama, as it builds up its almost unbearable tension and then releases it in a thunderous denouement.

Drama of confrontation

The previous Act ended with the warning of a cross and the promise of a crown (16:21-28). Now, in a final sweeping crescendo of word and movement, we learn how Jesus went to that cross and won that crown. The action takes us through successive scenes located on a high mountain, in Capernaum, on a journey beyond Jordan, and then into Jerusalem (chapters 17-20).

The 'Palm Sunday entry' to the capital (chapter 21) casts the spotlight on those dramatic symbolic actions; the ride on the donkey, the ejection of the merchants from the temple, and the cursing of the fig-tree (each action breathtaking in its Old Testament significance).[1]

---

1. Entry into Jerusalem: compare, for example, Zechariah 9:9, 14:4 and 14:21, and bear in mind that 'canaanite' may be translated 'merchant'. The fig tree was both a familiar symbol of Israel, and a place (under its thick shade) where devout people would pray and reflect on their knowledge of God – see John 1:47-51.

Here is *Kingship* of a new kind; the sovereign riding on a meek donkey, welcomed by happy children, and occupied with healing the sick in the temple courts.

But here is also *confrontation*, in a devastating series of parables, denunciations and apocalyptic visions, culminating in the fearful words, 'Then they will go away to eternal punishment, but the righteous to eternal life' (25:46). A constant theme in these chapters is that of the kingdom offered but rejected, and then offered to others who will delightedly welcome it: '... the kingdom of God will be taken away from you and given to a people who will produce its fruit' (21:43).

Here too is *purposeful direction*. A farewell supper, pregnant with meaning for past and future, agony in the moonlit garden, betrayal, arrest and trial; all are recorded with economy of detail and simple dignity. 'The path of the King' is not one on which he is forced by events, but one which he pursues with quiet purpose. 'The Son of Man will go just as it is written about him' (26:24). It must happen this way. The crucifixion is related with the same stark simplicity, yet woven with the same strands of purpose, sovereignty, confrontation and choices made (chapter 27).

Here again is *Kingship*, but not as the world understands the term. A mocking robe and a thorny crown, placarded words and shouted cat-calls; all bear ironic unintended witness to a suffering sovereign.

'He saved others,' they said, 'but he can't save himself! He's the king of Israel! Let him come down now from the cross, and we will believe in him' (27:42).

'Now heal thyself, Physician; now come down.'
'Alas I did so, when I left my crown
And Father's smile for you, to feel his frown:
Was ever grief like mine?'   (George Herbert)

Here is *polarization*. Ever since wise men looked for an infant king and Herod tried to kill him, that polarization has marked Matthew's whole story. People are pressed by events to take sides. They see what they wish to see, and in their choices display what they wish to be. Pilate chooses compromise, and keeps his job. The crowd choose violent Barabbas and announce their priorities. The soldiers choose cruelty and turn their backs on pity. But there are other, opposite choices. The captain of the guard acknowledges deity. The watching women display loyalty. Joseph the tomb-owner offers hospitality. Each of these is a submission to Christ's sovereignty that displays remarkable faith and courage.

And finally, God bears his own witness, as he has done throughout the story. Three awesome supernatural events symbolise the fact that the King on the cross has indeed won a great victory and delivered his people from the dominion of death and darkness, to give them new life in his kingdom. The great dividing curtain of the temple is torn (for the way to God is now open). The earth quakes (for the foundations of life have been changed). The tombs break open (for death itself is to be conquered). In the words of a great prayer, Christ, through his death, has 'opened the kingdom of heaven to all believers'.[2]

One more scene (Matthew 25). Dawn steals into the garden where the body lay entombed. And light for a new everlasting day dawns. No parable this; no abstract belief in survival after death, dressed up in mythological clothes. Matthew emphasises hard physical facts. The exact details match those of Friday's death-scene: what was physical then cannot be symbolic and vaguely 'spiritual' now.

The 'props' on the stage of the drama are still the same. There were *linen cloths*, and now they are unwrapped. There

---

2. The *Te Deum*, 'We praise you, oh God' which dates from sixth-century Rome. Verse 17 in the Alternative Service Book, 1980, version says:
When thou hadst overcome the sharpness of death
Thou didst open the kingdom of heaven to all believers.

was *a great heavy stone*, and now it has been rolled back. There was *an occupied tomb*, and now it is empty. There were *guards posted*, and now they are prostrate with terror. Women watched *the burial* and now they look in an empty grave. They were 'looking for Jesus who was crucified'. Now 'he is not here – but he is risen – see the place where he lay'.

The utter absurdity of the later account given by the bribed guards only emphasizes one fact: there really was an empty tomb that needed to be explained. Sleeping guards (when the penalty was death), cunning disciples (who move tons of stone without waking them!), and an eyewitness account ('we were there when it happened – fast asleep'!); all underline how many incredible things one must believe in order not to be a Christian.

And finally, the curtain, having fallen, rises again briefly and we have an *epilogue* that matches and balances the Christmas prologue. Wise men once came from the far places of the non-Jewish world, seeking the one born to be king of the Jews. Now that full-grown King, on the far side of death and resurrection, stands clothed with 'all authority in heaven and on earth'. He sends his disciples out to 'all the nations' to declare his sovereignty and his salvation. His right to rule the nations is his sacrifice offered for all. Because the price for all has been paid and God's 'Received with thanks' written over the empty cross and the empty tomb, all may come under his loving, saving sovereignty.

What, then, is Matthew telling us? That Jesus came to fulfil God's pledged purposes. That history does not go round in circles but moves towards a terminus and a destination. That the key to understanding is to see Jesus at the centre, bringing God's rule into people's hearts, suffering death to bring us life.

Gospel for today
We live in a world approaching a 'third millennium' since Christ was born. It is a world that has lost its way. Two great

human philosophies committed to 'destiny' and 'the inexorable process of history' have in this century brought almost inconceivable suffering, terror and disillusionment (the ugly opposites of fascism and communism). Both of them had a cancer at their heart: commitment to mankind without God.

Then is there no philosophy that can make sense of concepts like the march of history and the direction of human progress? Matthew tells us: not a philosophy and not strictly a religion either. God has a purpose. It is worked out, not through the rise and fall of nations and political or religious dogmas (wild beasts indeed), but through the True Man who is God's commissioned King, bringing a rule that begins in hearts surrendered to God. His is the everlasting dominion that shall not end (Daniel 7:14 quoted, remember, by Jesus at his trial). His is the authority that commissions his people to conquer 'all nations' by discipling them and teaching them all that he commanded (28:19-20).

This is the reasoning behind Matthew's love for the word 'fulfilled'. This is why he finds ingenious parallels between Jesus and the Old Testament characters and commands. In the words of a modern Matthean scholar, we are invited to 'sit with Matthew in his study ... and come to see that he is not playing slick word games, but rather exploring with reverent delight the sometimes unexpected links which emerge as *the same God who acted in the story of Israel* and who spoke through the prophets *now brings his redemptive schemes to fruition*' (my italics).[3]

Here, in very truth, is the one 'born to be King' – and not only for the Jew, but for the whole world. Those airport officials had good reason to pause and reflect!

---

3. R.T. France, *Matthew - Evangelist and Teacher*, p. 184. I owe many of the insights in my three chapters on Matthew to this brilliant, scholarly and reverent exploration of Matthew's Gospel.

Luke

Chapter 10

LUKE – MASTER OF STORY
AND HISTORY

Luke dominates the verbal landscape of the New Testament. He shapes our thinking about *Jesus and his church* more than any other writer. Notice my phrase. Others tell us more about Christ or more about his church. But Luke uniquely links history and theology to tell us about Christ *and* his church.

What we call Luke's Gospel is the nearest that we have to a biography of Jesus (though still a long way short of that). What we call the Acts of the Apostles is the nearest we have to a history of the early church. And the two are connected inseparably. They constitute Parts One and Two of one connected narrative.

In a striking phrase the writer refers back to Part One as 'all that Jesus *began* to do and to teach' (Acts 1:1). The clear implication is that Part Two will describe how he *continued*. And so it does. The ascended Christ works through his new-born church. The acts of the apostles are the continuing acts of Jesus, risen, ascended and Spirit-giving.

Familiar tales
It is Luke who records most of the best-known stories of Jesus. Not by mere coincidence do we find that the two most powerful modern film versions of Jesus' life and work draw heavily from Luke.[1]

---

1. Franco Zeffirelli's TV film *Jesus of Nazareth*, shown nationwide, and the Campus Crusade film, *Jesus*, distributed worldwide.

Without him, most of the best-loved parables would be lost to us. The Prodigal Son, the Good Samaritan, the Great Feast, the Rich Man and Lazarus, the Foolish Farmer; all come from Christ's lips but Luke's pen.

Where would the Christmas story be without Luke? No overbooked inn, no manger, no shepherds, no angels...

The three earliest liturgical hymns (or canticles) are preserved by Luke. Mary's *Magnificat*, Zechariah's *Benedictus*, and Simeon's *Nunc Dimittis* are sung or repeated daily in cathedral and monastic worship. All come to us via Luke.

Here is the first New Testament writer to compose a book for widespread formal publication, couched in a polished literary style, and addressed to an influential patron or sponsor. This was a book written according to the classical approach of the professional writer of his day. All of this is spelled out in the distinctive 'Preface' with which his book opens. The style and manner of his first paragraph signal his purpose and his viewpoint as surely as the introduction to an Arthur Bryant history or a collection of historical essays by A. J. P. Taylor. Here is polished narrative; selected, arranged and introduced in order to bring out a particular understanding of certain events.

Two books in one?
Something else makes Luke's Gospel distinct from the others. His story of Jesus is only half of the book. It continues with the great drama of the church's early days. And the two scrolls between them fill one quarter of the New Testament.

I mention 'scrolls' deliberately. A book in the first century did not consist of separate pages glued together at the spine. The pages were sewn together side by side in a continuous strip and rolled up 'sideways' for storage. Luke's 'Life of Christ' is roughly the maximum possible length and bulk for a manageable scroll. His 'Life of the Church' is a similar length. When a book was that long, it was split into two scrolls. The first usually began with an explanatory prologue, called a *proem*. The second scroll picked up the threads with a shorter preface. This is exactly how Luke's work is constructed. Recognising this essential unity, modern scholars increasingly refer to the whole work as Luke-Acts, and write joint commentaries on the one book. In fact it is not two books in one, as my subtitle suggests, but one book in two!

A comparison with the Jewish historian Josephus (late first century) is fascinating. This military commander of Galilee who changed sides and subsequently rose high in Roman circles, is best known to Christians for his rather enigmatic references to Jesus and John the Baptist. He wrote a less-known book in reply to one Apion who was slandering his Jewish ancestors.[2] This too was lengthy, and filled two scrolls. The resemblance between Luke and Josephus is striking. Both address their books to 'his excellency' (one called Theophilus, the other Epaphroditus). Both give their reason for writing; to get the facts straight. Both address their influential friend again in the first sentence of their second volume. Both are careful to present the characters in their work as no threat to Rome. The resemblance is really not strange at all, for both were deliberately writing *history*, as that exercise was understood in their time.

So here is another 'first' for Luke. He writes the first Christian history. In doing so, he follows the method of Thucydides, regarded by many as the father of scientific history (which means, of course, not a history of science, but a careful gathering of facts as opposed to edifying fable).[3]

The method involved the sifting or discarding of mere folk-

---

2. See *Luke-Acts* by Donald Juel, for the comparison with Josephus, *Against Apion*. The double-title for Luke's one work seems to have been used first by Henry Cadbury of Harvard, in his book *The Making of Luke-Acts*.
3. Thucydides. See I. Howard Marshall, *The Acts of the Apostles*, p. 42.

lore and adulatory stories. Letters, diaries, reports and eyewitness accounts were pursued. As much as possible was checked
out by visits to the appropriate sites, and interviews with
people whose reminiscences could be examined.

The historian then anchored his gathered facts to some
recognisable period in time by linking them with known
figures and events like the reign of an emperor, the appoint-
ment of a governor, the rise of a religious cult, the organising
of a census or the fighting of a battle.[4]

This is exactly what Luke does. He explains his method in
his 'proem', usually called Luke's Prologue (1:1-4). There he
refers to earlier documents ('many have undertaken to draw
up an account'). He points to first-hand testimony ('those who
from the first were eyewitnesses'). He describes his own
'careful investigations'. Out of this he offers an 'orderly
account'.

Time and place

The time-anchor he then fixes as the reign of 'Herod, King of
Judaea' and 'the days of Caesar Augustus', and 'the first
census while Quirinius was governor of Syria' (1:5 and 2:1-
2). This last note offers scope for endless speculation amongst
scholars from the second century to the twentieth, since the
governor does not 'fit' too well.[5]

When Jesus is adult, and commences his public ministry,
Luke again anchors the story to known historical figures:

---

4. The method (as adopted by Luke) is explained in detail by David
Gooding in his splendid book, *According to Luke*. He also expounds
in detail the way in which Luke follows Aristotle's method of setting
two or three successive stories in contrast or comparison, so that a
powerful point is made by suggestion instead of direct statement.

5. Tertullian, Christian lawyer and preacher in the second century,
described Sentius Satutninus as governor in Syria during the 'Christmas census'. Quirinius (Luke's character) was in fact a military commander at that point, but *later became governor*, so Luke's use of his
name is quite allowable. See further comments in the Appendix.

Tiberius was emperor, Pilate was Judaean governor, another Herod was puppet-king of Galilee, Annas and Caiaphas were high priests in Jerusalem (3:1-3). This focuses the chronology considerably: we are looking at a period around AD 28 or slightly later.[6]

Apart from these figures, who all appear in secular history, the Gospel account offers us little. Judaea was a fairly obscure province on the outer rim of the Roman Empire. With Acts, things are different. The story moves steadily across the Mediterranean world through major cities, overlapping with other known events, and climaxing in Rome, the heart of the civilised world. It can be checked, confirmed and correlated at several points. For example, Paul's friends and fellow church-planters Aquila and Priscilla were expelled from Rome in a purge about which we have 'outside information' (Acts 18:1-3). Gallio was indeed Proconsul of Achaia in 51-52 so we can fix Paul's stay there (Acts 18:12-17). A splendid little touch in the dramatic account of the riot in Ephesus is provided by the City Clerk whose tactful speech refers to 'proconsuls' (plural). A city could only have one proconsul. But history tells us of a dispute between two claimants to the office at that time: the wily local official keeps his options open and acknowledges both of them! (Acts 19:37-41).

Sure facts

I could continue almost indefinitely. Luke's second scroll can be checked for accuracy at numerous points. Therefore we have every reason to believe that the first scroll (his Gospel) is accurate too. To the devout Christian none of this may seem terribly important, as what we are looking at is God's inspired word, 'true' by definition and not needing to be argued. On the other hand, the form in which God chooses to give any particular part of his revelation is a clue to the nature of what is being revealed. Matthew was inspired to record blocks of

---

6. For a suggested chronology, see Appendix.

teaching, which is one medium of truth. Mark gives eyewitness memoirs and that is another; Luke's careful research
reminds us forcefully that God oversees the march of history,
and has stepped into its stream in the person of our Lord Jesus
Christ. What Luke gives us in both halves of his book might
be called *a theology of history*.

A nineteenth and twentieth-century scholar, explorer and
archaeologist, Sir William Ramsay, has confirmed all of this:

> 'Luke's statement of facts are trustworthy; he is possessed
> of the true historic sense; he fixes his mind on the plan ...
> and proportions the scale of his treatment to the importance
> of each detail.'[7]

This testimony is all the more impressive because Ramsay
begins his investigation with the opposite assumption; that
Luke used the appearance of history as a vehicle of his
predetermined beliefs, and 'described' events as he felt they
should have happened,[8] thereby creating (in effect) *a history
of theology* (something quite different). But the sheer weight
of evidence caused the scholar to acknowledge Luke as a
superb historian.

Who was Luke?

From the beginning, church authorities have held to the
traditional authorship. Luke, they affirm, was the 'beloved
physician' who joined Paul's evangelistic team and is referred
to in several apostolic letters (Colossians 4:14; 2 Timothy 4:
9-11; Philemon 23 and 24). In Acts itself he seems to appear

---

7. Sir William Ramsay wrote a whole succession of books on the subject of
Luke and Paul. The quotation is from *The Bearing of Recent Discovery on
the Trustworthiness of the New Testament*, p. 222. His best-known and most-
quoted work was *St. Paul, The Traveller and Roman Citizen* (1895).
8. The view that Luke made up his 'history' to suit his theology is still held
by some modern critics. It is examined at length – and rejected – by I.
Howard Marshall in *Luke – Historian and Theologian*, Chapter 3.

anonymously in the famous 'We-Passages', where the author speaks in the third person plural. It first happens in mid-paragraph at a vital point in Paul's second great mission journey: '*They* passed by Mysia and went down to Troas. During the night Paul had a vision .... After Paul had seen the vision, *we* got ready at once to leave for Macedonia' (Acts 16: 8-10, emphasis mine).

The writer, it seems, has come on board (quite literally!). He writes himself into the story, because at that point he personally entered the events. What follows is significant: we read one of the most vivid episodes in the New Testament. The church is planted in the Roman colony of Philippi, its first converts and members being a Jewish businesswoman, a pagan slave-girl and a Roman soldier. In the colourful details we see, surely, the marks of personal recollection.

The same thing happens several times.[9] The word 'we' re-appears as an introduction to a vividly detailed account: most noticeably with the great storm-and-shipwreck story, with its technical details of geography, weather and nautical action.

The likeliest explanation for all this is that the writer joined the evangelistic team and then left again, at various points, presumably to continue his medical work, until eventually the battered and ailing Paul needed him permanently as private doctor. The actual 'we passages', I assume, are quoted verbatim from Luke's personal journal or diary, exactly in accord with his historian's method of using eyewitness material.

If we accept all this (and it is widely assumed) then we can even see the point at which his writing project became possible. He would find himself kicking his heels in Roman Caesarea, on the coast of Judaea, whilst Paul languished in jail for five years because of a misunderstanding (Acts 23: 22-29 and 24:27). What better time and place to begin research for his double volume. Here he was, in the land of Jesus, able to

---

9. The 'We Passages' of Acts are 16:10-17; 20: 5-15; 21: 1-18 and chapters 27 and 28.

talk to people who had known or heard the Saviour. Here too was material from the infancy of the Jerusalem church. Here (one assumes) he could even talk to Mary the mother of Jesus. (Tradition even assures us that he painted her portrait!)

Putting it together

Here, then, is the likely scenario: Luke was probably a non-Jew, and a convert of the Gentile Mission. Unexpectedly, he had time on his hands in the Holy Land. He was a doctor, trained to diagnose and to sift evidence. He had a command of literary Greek. But we must be careful not to exaggerate: a doctor in the Roman Empire had neither the skills nor the education nor even the reputation of modern physicians. We are not to imagine a kind of first-century Dr. Martyn Lloyd-Jones!

Nevertheless, he represented a new Christian generation. What he lacked in personal knowledge of the Jesus-events, he made up for in access to research and information. Added to that was, of course, the divine inspiration which moved and informed him.

Compared with the other Gospel writers, he approached the great events from the opposite end, so to speak. The others were Jews, residents of Jerusalem or Galilee, and personal followers of Jesus in 'the days of his flesh'. Luke was a foreigner, a non-Jew who had never met Christ personally; a convert of an evangelist who had not met him before his resurrection either. Obviously he must approach the task from a different angle, and handle it in a different way. How he did that, we can now consider, by examining Luke's style, construction, material and very obvious theology. Most important of all, we shall see Jesus as he is understood by a second-generation disciple. Here, presented with winsome eloquence is *the Saviour of the world*.

Chapter 11

JESUS, SAVIOUR AND LORD

Luke's Gospel is the air that evangelical Christians breathe. Here is a glowing picture of Jesus *the Saviour*. Here is spelled out the message of undeserved, gracious saving love. Here is the Christ who came to seek and to save the lost.

In the earliest chapters of the 'Christmas Story' we hear people and angels speaking and singing of 'the Saviour', 'salvation', 'Good news of great joy'.[1]

As the book begins, so it continues. The verb *sozo* (to save) occurs seventeen times, and related verbs in the same abundance.[2] One of the writer's most obvious delights is to tell conversion stories of how people came to saving faith in Jesus. Zacchaeus, the penitent thief, Saul of Tarsus, the Philippian jailer (for the same is seen in the second scroll too): the attentive reader will find many other examples.[3] This is no less true of the parables which abound in Luke's account, and make him surely the most-quoted Gospel writer. They could well be labelled 'Conversion Parables'. How many evangelistic appeals have been based on the stories of the rich fool who neglected his soul, the great banquet to which the first invited guests declined to come, and the three 'lost-and-found-tales'

---

1. 'The Christmas Gospel' (Luke 1: 46-47, 67-69; 2: 10-11 and 28-32).
2. 'Saved': some examples are Luke 7:50; 8:12; 13:23; 19:10. Admittedly, Mark and Matthew also use this word quite freely but give it the widest sense of 'rescue' or 'healing'. Luke almost invariably means forgiveness and restoration to God. Even more strikingly, Luke alone amongst Gospel writers uses the words 'salvation' and 'Saviour' (8 times in Luke and 9 in Acts.)
3. Conversion Stories (Luke 19: 1-10; 23: 39-43; Acts 9: 1-19; 16: 1-34).

of the sheep, the coin and the prodigal son?

In my first pastorate I used to take Communion to an old Presbyterian too frail to attend church. One day he related his conversion to me; it had taken place only ten years earlier when a young preacher had rented the Territorial Army drill hall in his village, and preached a series of sermons on these very parables. To our mutual astonishment, I realised that I was that preacher! As a person, I had left no impression on his memory, but the parables recorded by Luke had changed his life.[4]

In his matchless 'epilogue' of resurrection appearances, Luke sums up the theme himself. Jesus explains to his bewildered disciples:

> This is what is written. The Christ will suffer and rise from the dead on the third day, and repentance and forgiveness of sins will be preached in his name to all nations (24: 46-47).

Skilful storytelling

The writer's literary style underlines the saving message. Employing masterly classical Greek, in what Ernst Renan has called 'the most beautiful book ever written', Luke reveals himself as an evangelist as well as a theologian and a historian. He adapts the style pioneered by Thucydides, setting contrasting or comparative stories side by side to make his point at an almost subliminal level. And Luke's point is always this: Jesus came to save the lost and find the wanderer.

The story falls into three obvious sections, very disparate in length. First we read of *the coming of the Saviour* (chapters 1 and 2). The Nativity Stories of Jesus' birth and childhood are written in a style all their own, almost quaintly pious and Jewish.

The style abruptly changes with the second section: *the call*

---

4. Conversion Parables: Luke 12: 13-21 (the Rich Fool); 14: 15-24 (the Great Banquet); 15:11-32 (the Prodigal Son); 16:19-31 (the Rich Man and Lazarus).

of the Saviour. Jesus' adult and public ministry is portrayed with haunting skill (chapters 3-8). The emphasis is different, as well as the style. The repeated theme is that of Christ's totally gracious love. No-one deserves his grace; but then grace, by definition, is undeserved! The story of the Roman centurion's faith offers one striking illustration (7:1-10). Jewish leaders approach Jesus on his behalf: 'This man deserves to have you [heal his servant] because he ... built our synagogue.' But that is not the man's own view: 'I did not even consider myself *worthy* to come to you. But say the word and my servant will be healed.' The Son of God brings unmerited aid from the Father. It is the message that Luke has seen in action wherever he travelled with the apostle Paul!

The third section occupies the rest of the Gospel (chapters 9 to 24), a huge proportion of the whole. I call it *the journey of the Saviour.* Bible scholars of all shades of opinion refer to it as 'The Journey Narrative'. It introduces its theme in the words of 9:51: 'As the time approached for him to be taken up to heaven, Jesus resolutely set out for Jerusalem.'

That phrase, or something very like it, is repeated at least seven times (perhaps more).[5] A journey is under way. It has a destination. Strictly speaking, the destination is heaven's glory (notice the verse just quoted). The last stop but one is more often spoken of: the city of Jerusalem, where Jesus will suffer, die and rise again, to open the way to glory for all who trust in him.

This journey (with its double meaning and double destination on earth and in heaven) dominates the story and gathers up within it most of the uniquely Lukan episodes and parables. Weaving in and out amongst its episodes are those Greek contrast stories to which I have referred. Here, without doubt, is the central motif of Luke's Jesus-story.

---

5. The Journey Narrative (Luke 9: 52-57; 10:1, 38; 13:22, 32, 33; 17:11; 19:1, 11, 28. Some of these do not mention Jerusalem as the destination, but emphasise the urgent sense of direction.

First, the journey is *geographical*. It really does begin in
one place (northern Galilee) and end in another (Jerusalem),
a hundred miles south. But it encompasses some geographical
puzzles. There were two alternative routes possible. Steadily
southwards across the hills of Samaria ran the ancient Patriarchs' Way; the route followed by Abraham, Isaac and Jacob
and still a switchback road to this day. Less direct was the road
eastward across the river Jordan at the southern end of Galilee,
and southwards along the eastern bank of the river through
what was then the province of Peraea. This route (avoiding the
unpleasant and mocking Samaritans) re-crosses the river
again at Jericho.

The geographical problem is that Luke takes us along both
routes, and to places in succession which seem to make no
sense of one consecutive journey. At times we are in Samaria,
at times in Peraea. Most confusing of all, only halfway through
the journey in terms of time, Jesus visits his friends in Bethany,
just a day's walk from Jerusalem.[6]

This puzzle introduces a second possibility. The journey is
perhaps to be seen as a *literary device*, Luke has a lot of new
material (not referred to by Mark or Matthew). Perhaps he puts
it all together under the general category of 'things that Jesus
said and did on his way to Jerusalem, suffering and death'?
Perhaps, by repeating at intervals the theme of 'Face set
toward Jerusalem' he gives a unifying theme to what is
otherwise a miscellaneous collection of incidents and parables. Many modern scholars assume this to be the case, and
there is some merit in it. It is a perfectly legitimate way to
compose a composite picture of a complex person.

However, I find this unsatisfying if it stands alone, and want
to further suggest an *evangelistic* purpose that combines the
first two explanations. The clue is found in the way the journey

6. Puzzling points on the journey: 9:52 (Samaria), 10:38 (Bethany, cf.
John 12:1), 17:11 (the border between Samaria and Galilee), 18:35
(approaching Jericho).

begins. 'After this the Lord appointed seventy-two others and
sent them two by two ahead of him to every town and place
where he was about to go' (10:1). There follows a detailed
account of the way this mission was carried out (10:2-12), and
a lament over the Galilean towns where previous missions had
been held (10:13-16). The seventy-two return with a 'jubilant'
report of their successes, and Jesus responds with words of
deep import about the conflict with evil, the certainty of
heaven, and the assurance that the Father reveals his saving
truth to those who place their simple trust in him (10:17-24).

What does this now suggest? The 'Journey to Jerusalem'
took the form of an extended series of heralding missions,
some taken by the seventy-two, some by the twelve, and some
by Jesus himself. It had Jerusalem (and heaven!) as its
eventual destination and climax.

Once that is understood, the geographical anomalies are no
longer a muddle or a mystery. In order to cover 'every town
and place', they would zigzag between both alternative routes,
along the east-west roads through smaller valleys that can still
be traced today (indeed I have traced them with car, map,
Bible, and occasional use of binoculars, where barbed wire
intervenes!).[7] As for the seemingly anomalous arrival in
Bethany halfway through the story, one of those striking
unintended coincidences that we shall find in John's account,
offers the solution. John does in fact place Jesus 'almost
there', when he visits Bethany to raise his friend Lazarus from
the tomb – and then withdraws northwards and westwards
again for several months, before his Palm Sunday ride into the
capital (John 11: 45-57).

Now we have, I suggest, three explanations of the Journey
Narrative and its significance: geographical, literary and
evangelistic. My fourth binds them together, and is psycho-
logical, metaphorical and spiritual. Let me suggest a modern

---

7. For a suggested chronology of Christ's three-year ministry, see
Appendix.

analogy. Harold Macmillan was a powerful British political figure after the Second World War. His grandparents began life in poverty on the island of Arran, off the west coast of Scotland. His father's first mainland job was selling Bibles and books door-to-door, from which he and his brother built up the international publishing business of Macmillans. Harold himself turned to politics and, pursuing a fascinating zigzag course, eventually became Prime Minister at a critical moment of British history, after the 'Suez affair'.

Now it would be possible to write his story from that midway point of the decision to enter politics, and entitle it 'From Highland Cottage to Downing Street'. An alternative title might be 'The Road to Westminster'. Those phrases would have a double meaning. *Geographically* it is true that the journey began in Arran and ended in London. *Metaphorically*, it was a moral and political journey. In neither sense was it a journey in a straight line. At times he was geographically further away from London than he was at the beginning, and moving yet further away as he travelled. Yet it was always the road to Westminster, the route to Downing Street.[8]

The Jerusalem Journey was infinitely more significant, but the illustration I find helpful. What made it a *Salvation* journey has still to be explored. For, as I have shown, Jerusalem was not really the destination after all. There is yet another strand to the story.

---

8. I owe this helpful analogy to David Gooding in his *According to Luke*. He suggests an American version, *From Log Cabin to White House*. I prefer a British equivalent!

Chapter 12

EATING WITH OUTCASTS

It is my guess that Luke has done more to shape the popular image of Jesus in the western world than any other writer. Here is the friend of sinners, the seeking shepherd, the welcomer of outcasts, the restorer of women's dignity, the man who breaks barriers, and the reformer who infuriated the complacent. These are the Lukan images that have shaped Christian thinking and illumined evangelical experience. Here are the basic ingredients of the experience of forgiveness and conversion. In a word, here is a book that tells us how Christ makes Christians.

It is Luke who delineates those characteristics of Jesus that we associate with *the gospel of grace*. God offers mankind his salvation, not because we deserve it or can hope to earn it, but simply because we desperately need it.

Perhaps one picture painted by Luke most vividly portrays Jesus the Saviour, and most nearly approached one's desire to know what he was 'really like'. He is depicted as *The Man Who Eats with Outcasts*.

We see it in the famous introduction to the parable of the Prodigal Son:

Now the tax-collectors and 'sinners' were all gathering round to hear him. But the Pharisees and the teachers of the law muttered, 'This man welcomes sinners, and eats with them' (15:1-2).

This could lay claim to being the key sentence of Luke's Gospel. Jesus, he tells us, organised parties to proclaim his gospel of forgiveness, used banquet stories to illustrate the call of the kingdom, and caused shocked disapproval by the people he chose to eat with.

> Jesus ... saw a tax-collector by the name of Levi ... 'Follow me,' Jesus said .... Levi held a great banquet for Jesus at his house. [Jesus said] 'I have not come to call the righteous, but sinners to repentance.'

> 'People will come from east and west and north and south, and will take their places at the feast in the kingdom of God.'

> 'A certain man was preparing a banquet and invited many guests ...'[1]

Purpose and pattern

These are but three of very many references, that are built into the story with almost geometrical precision. Jesus accepts a meal with a strictly kosher Pharisee and has some sharp things to say about true purity. The tale is told of a successful farmer who coins the phrase 'eat, drink and be merry', and then drops dead. Disciples are warned not to worry unduly about food and clothing. A whole run of parables about the need for watchfulness; all involve meals.[2]

Then follow the most famous parables that are unique to Luke's account. All invoke the theme of 'people lost and found'. Most involve meals. The Great Banquet (to which the complacent refuse to come); the Prodigal Son (who is given a welcome-home feast which his self-righteous brother refuses to attend); the Rich Man and Lazarus (the first of whom feasts in this life but thirsts in the next): all point up the same lesson and all use the analogy of meal-tables.[3]

That does not exhaust the theme. As Jesus approaches the climax of that meal-studded journey, he pauses to invite

---

1. *The meal motif*: Luke 5: 27-32; 13: 29-30; 14: 16-24.
2. *More meal stories*: Luke 11: 37-41; 12: 13-21; 12: 22-34.
3. *The Salvation Parables*: Luke 14: 15-23; Luke 15; Luke 16: 19-31.

himself as guest to the chief inspector of taxes in Jericho. 'He
has gone to be guest of a sinner,' the people object. 'Today
salvation has come to his house,' is Christ's reply (19:1-10).

A few days later, in Jerusalem, a new kind of meal is
organised. Passover approaches. Rabbi and friends recline at
the loaded table, half-lying around the low three-branched
triclinium table in that position suggestive of freedom and
assurance which contrasted with the threat and taste of the very
first Passover.[4] Then the meaning and message are developed
and transformed. A body given ... new covenant pledged in
blood ... bread and wine ... a call to 'remembrance' which
means much more than mere recollection. Once more it is a
meal which spotlights, symbolises and conveys the purpose of
saving grace for sinners.

> Thy presence makes the feast;
> Now may our spirits feel
> The glory not to be expressed,
> The joy unspeakable   (Charles Wesley).

The unfolding story is not yet complete, nor is the journey
ended. At the cross, even as the entry-price to God's Banquet
is being paid by the suffering Son, a dying thief turns in
penitence and despair to Christ, and is assured of a place at the
Palace Garden Party (23:39-43. 'Paradise' means literally 'the
king's garden').

Now follows another journey that culminates in another
meal. Two people, staggering with grief and burdened with
broken hopes, are overtaken on their homeward trudge by the

---

4. *Passover Customs*: Luke 22:7-23, cf. Exodus 12:1-11. Originally the
Israelites were fleeing slaves, now they were free and in their promised
land. The distinction is important for Christian understanding of Holy
Communion. The reclining position, of course, made possible the 'foot
washing' which John chooses to record at the same meal (John 13:1-17).
Art has almost invariably failed to reflect this, and so has to position the
twelve in various peculiar attitudes to fit the many ingredients in the story.

risen but unrecognised Lord. He explains how a suffering Christ is a necessary prelude to 'entering his glory'. Uncomprehending, but warmed in heart, they invite him to their evening meal (seed-thought for Henry Lyte's hymn, *Abide with me, fast falls the eventide*). He 'says grace' as he 'breaks the bread' ... and they recognise him.[5]

It all encapsulates the experience of Christians throughout the ages (and expresses the deepest convictions of this present writer, if I may say so). In ministry of Word and Sacrament (these not rivals but allies), the Living Christ walks with his believing people, and conducts them to heaven.

At the King's table

'Eating together' held enormous significance in Palestine during the time that Luke describes. To pious Jews, what you ate, how you prepared it and with whom you ate it, were symbolic declarations of what it meant to be the People of God. The rescue operation that had made them a Covenant People itself involved a meal.

By Jesus' time, Pharisaical fastidiousness had dangerously externalised the whole concept and given it a complacent self-righteous and superficial significance. Your diet and table-company became the very essence of your place in the Covenant. From that table-company many (even most) were automatically excluded. Lepers because of illness, tax collectors because of profession, women because of gender, Samaritans because of religion, Gentiles because of race, even Galileans because of dialect; all of these were marginalised, despised and excluded.

Then along came Jesus and (pardon the phrase) turned the tables. By eating with doubtful characters, teaching truth in his table-talk, and claiming the Messianic banquet-promise for himself, he declared God's salvation for all, irrespective of race, religion or status. The message was clear. God welcomes

---

5. 'The journey to Emmaus' (Luke 24: 13-35).

people to the provision made by his Son ... and on the sole basis of their need and their willing response. The only thing that can keep you out is the arrogant idea that you have a right to come in.[6]

This, then, is the theme of the Journey Narrative. It is more than that: it provides Luke's basic picture of Jesus the Saviour. It will be repeated in the 'second half' of his book, which we call *Acts*. There are fascinating parallels, too numerous to pursue here in detail.

The story told again

Acts, too, has a strongly Jewish 'Infancy Narrative', but the infant is now the new-born church. Acts too has its turning-point in a recognition of Jesus as Messiah, Saviour and Lord (the recognition is now not Peter's but Paul's). From that critical point, Acts too tells of a Journey Narrative. Now the destination is not Jerusalem but Rome, which is reached in the final chapter.[7] The journey (of the missionaries) is filled with examples of conversion, as one despised people-group after another embraces a universal gospel. And meals have their place too, as symbols of the barrier-breaking message. The Jerusalem Church has a daily table-fellowship (2:42-47). The vision of a kosher-breaking meal shocks Peter into a willingness to take the message to Gentiles (10:1-23, 44-48). A serious threat to the universality of grace is averted by agreeing on 'who eats with whom' (15:1-21). The breaking of bread on the first day of the week replaces the Sabbath-meals on the seventh (20:7). And the final picture of an evangelising church in Rome, the world's capital, shows Paul, having completed his journey, using a rented house where 'all were welcome' as he preached boldly and without hindrance.

---

6. Isaiah 25:6-9 was one of the most commonly-quoted Messianic banquet promises. For the whole theme of 'Christ eating with sinners' see *Jesus, the Man and His Message*, chapter 3.

7. By a pleasant coincidence (for chapters were not included in the original scroll) the turning-point in both books is in their ninth chapters.

Evangelist, theologian and historian

I began by calling Luke a superb historian. So he is, but that is not his principal purpose. He is not recording objective neutrally informative history (is there really such a thing?). He is recording facts in the service of faith. His narrative is the story of *the progress of Christ's gospel*: first through the life and death of God's Son, and then through the life and witness of Christ's Church.

We do not finish the book by exclaiming, 'Now I know all the facts about Jesus', but rather by crying, 'Here is my Saviour, and he may be yours too.' We do not conclude with the thought, 'Now I understand early Church history', but rather with the awed reflection, 'This Saviour is still at work by his Spirit, in his Church.'

John

Chapter 13

JOHN – THEOLOGY LIT BY LOVE

The Fourth Gospel soars like an eagle. That noble bird was quickly invoked as an apt symbol of John's Gospel; a book described as 'the most treasured possession of the Christian Church'.[1]

Just when we may be feeling that we are starting to grasp what a 'Gospel' is supposed to be, John compels us to think again. For his work is in a class of its own; a shining sword honed to a perfect cutting edge.

In a famous remark puzzled over ever since, an early Christian writer called this the 'spiritual Gospel'. The first church historian, Eusebius, quotes Clement the bishop of Alexandria around 200 as saying:

> John, last of all, conscious that the outward facts had been set forth in the Gospels ... divinely moved by the Spirit, composed a spiritual Gospel.[2]

Thirteen centuries later, the Protestant reformer John Calvin wrote something strikingly similar:

> John emphasises (more than the others) the *doctrine* in which Christ's office and the power of his death and resurrection are explained.... The first three exhibit his body, if I may be permitted to put it like that, but John shows his soul.[3]

---

1. Bishop John Charles Ryle (1816-1900) in his Introduction to *Notes on the Gospel of St. John.*
2. Eusebius, *Ecclesiastical History* 6: 14:7.
3. John Calvin, *Commentary on John*, 1:6.

Three centuries later again, the brash and bustling English city of Liverpool was given its first Anglican bishop, J. C. Ryle. He described John as 'pre-eminently full of things hard to understand'. Writing a three-volume commentary designed for lay people to read aloud in their parish sick-visiting (!), he explained that John was full of profound statements about 'the divinity of Christ, salvation by faith, the work of the Holy Ghost, and the privileges of believers'.[4] Here, clearly, is something more than a collection of stories about Jesus!

In the beginning

John's opening words transport his readers into a world of sublime concepts and awesome absolutes. Professor C. E. M. Joad, a regular broadcaster on the BBC 'Brain's Trust' (a 1940s predecessor of programmes like 'Any Questions'), was once asked to quote the most profound words ever written. He was renowned for his slightly sardonic agnosticism, but in actual fact was feeling his way towards Christian faith. After a moment's hesitation, he solemnly recited words from John's 'prologue': 'The Word became flesh and dwelt among us, and we beheld his glory.'

Like the rest of the book, that opening statement defied definition. What exactly *is* it? A sermon? A poem? A creed? A theological position-paper? An act of worship?

People who met Jesus

One way to look at the book is to see it as a collection of *interviews*. Here is the Sue Lawley or Jonathan Dimbleby of the first century, summoning one 'personality' after another to tell viewers and listeners how he or she first encountered Jesus, and came to the conclusion that he is the Son of God.

This is not a facile illustration. Roy Clements of Cambridge preached a series of outstanding evangelistic sermons

---

4. Ryle in his Introduction to *Notes on the Gospel of St. John.*

from this Gospel, and then printed them as a powerful book of apologetics. He writes:

> The easiest way to understand the difference between John's Gospel and the other Gospels is to compare it to the difference between a chat show and the nine o'clock news. ... John wants us to meet Jesus in an intimate way ... and that means *conversation*.[5]

The characters who crowd John's pages are certainly as colourful and varied as those who appear on the chat shows! They have peopled the imagination and inspired the faith of Christians for twenty centuries. Here is Nathanael, whose reveries are interrupted by the discovery of a living ladder to heaven (chapter 1). Here is Nicodemus the religious leader, whose night-time visit uncovered his need for new birth (chapter 3). Here is the unnamed Samaritan woman who meets 'a man who told me everything I ever did' (chapter 4). Incidentally, their roles are strikingly reversed! The religious leader comes to discuss theology and is bluntly told that he needs conversion. The ill-reputed woman who obviously does need a new start is told something profound about the nature of worship!

There are so many others who meet Jesus and are never the same again. An anonymous blind man receives new sight and defies the bullying religious police with a kind of cheek born of dawning faith (chapter 9). Mary and Martha sob out their sorrow, and make a staggering discovery of Christ's power over death (chapter 11). Joseph of Arimathaea waits too long to declare his faith in Jesus ... and then discovers it is not too late after all (19:38). These people and others stride out of John's pages into Christian imagination and devotion.

---

5. Roy Clements, *Introducing Jesus*, p.13.

Christian movements through history
The Fourth Gospel (like Luke's) has always been a favourite
with Evangelicals. Older Christians can recall a time when
practically every child in the land knew by heart 'the gospel
in a nutshell', referred to simply as John Three Sixteen (AV):

> For God so loved the world that he gave his only begotten
> Son, that whosoever believeth in him, should not perish,
> but have everlasting life.

Almost everyone knew the Johannine phrase, 'Ye must be
born again'. Intriguingly, the words have gained fresh im-
pulse again in recent years: people know (or think they know)
what a 'born again' Christian is: so many sports personali-
ties, entertainers and media-people have taken the label!
    Less widely known amongst Evangelicals is the fact that
the Orthodox Christians of the East also draw their inspiration from John. Their almost mystical emphasis on life, im-
mortality and 'indwelling' stems from John. And by a curious geographical and historical twist, the early Celtic Church,
which first evangelised Ireland, Scotland, Northumbria and
northern Europe, was self-consciously Johannine. When, in
644, two great Christian movements met at Whitby to settle
once and for all whether Easter should be celebrated on Peter's choice of dates or John's (and whose hairstyle out of the
two should be adopted by missionary monks!), the issues
really went much deeper – and this writer may perhaps be
pardoned for suggesting that the wrong side won![6] Thus ancient monastic movements and the more modern Anglo-
Catholic influence equally claim to look to John for their
pattern of devotion.

---

6. The Synod of Whitby is often regarded as the climactic point in the
struggle for supremacy between the Celtic (Columban) Church who
evangelised northern England, and the Roman (Augustinian) Church
whose monasteries moved northwards from Kent. Rome prevailed.

It is he alone who records those great 'I am' sayings of Jesus. That fact gives a vital clue both to the style and the purpose of his Gospel. He, too, alone lists the seven 'signs', using a different word from the synoptists to describe Christ's miracles, and drawing from them profound meaning about the Son of God and his purpose in entering the world.

Is the picture coming together? John's is essentially a *theological and faith-promoting document*. He says so himself, in so many words ... both at the beginning and the end of his book.

> Yet to all who received [Christ] to those who believed in his name, he gave the right to become children of God ... born of God (John 1:12-13).

> These [events] are written that you may believe that Jesus is the Christ, the Son of God, and that by believing you may have life in his name (John 20:31).

The Good News Bible is, I suppose, Britain's pop-version of Scripture. Its introduction to the Fourth Gospel includes these words:

> ... the book tells how some people believed in Jesus, and became his followers, while others opposed him, and refused to believe ... John emphasizes the gift of eternal life through Christ, a gift that begins now and which comes to those who respond to Jesus.[7]

It would be hard to put it more succinctly.

Notice the words 'a gift that begins now'. This is the emphasis that has come to be described by theologians (whose business it is to think of splendidly obscure phrases) as *realised eschatology*. It is the teaching that, in Jesus, all of God's promises for the future find a 'now fulfilment', in the

---

7. Today's English Version, otherwise known as the Good News Bible.

believer's immediate heart-experience. What had been thought of as a distant prospect becomes wonderfully possible *now* for the believer, who receives, welcomes and 'abides in' the Son of God.

Judgment Day in the far-off future? But – 'Whoever believes in [the Son] is not condemned, but whoever does not believe stands *condemned already*' (3:18, emphasis mine).

Resurrection Day at some time beyond the horizon? But – 'I tell you the truth, a time is coming *and has now come* when the dead will hear the voice of the Son of God and those who hear will live' (5:25, emphasis mine).

Eternal Life as something to be entered either at the moment of death or at the Return of Christ? But – '*Now this is eternal life*: that they may know you, the only true God, and Jesus Christ, whom you have sent' (17:3, emphasis mine).

Variations on a theme
All of these quotations illustrate the constant, unchanging theme of this book. If it were not so magnificently written (and written about so magnificent a Person) one might be tempted to say that the writer has a one-track mind and expresses it with monotonous regularity! 'Jesus claims to be the Son of God, the Saviour of the world, the only Way to the Father. You either believe it or you don't. On that faith or unbelief, everything hangs.' This is a fair summary of John's ever-recurring theme.

Majestic in its simplicity but disturbing in its exclusiveness, that sums up the message of the Fourth Evangelist. But who was he?

A question of identity
The oldest tradition, apparently universally accepted, was that the writer was John the fisherman, brother of James, son of Zebedee, and one of the first to follow Christ. Like the other three, the Gospel is 'anonymous'. But it contains a special

collection of hints and clues. For whilst several disciple-apostles are mentioned by name (Andrew, Philip, Peter, Nathanael and Thomas), John's name is oddly absent, for one who was so centrally involved. Instead, an unnamed member of the group frequently appears, described either as 'another disciple' or as 'the disciple whom Jesus loved'.

We see BD (as scholars airily refer to the Beloved Disciple) amongst the first two to follow Jesus, in a position of trust during the Upper Room discussion, following Jesus at a distance when the Master was arrested, standing at the cross in the last moments, racing Peter to the empty tomb on Easter morning, and on the beach with Peter back in Galilee (John 1:35-40; 13:23; 18:15; 19:26; 20:1-9; 21:7-25). This man, we are told by the equally anonymous editor or sponsors of the Fourth Gospel, was the one who 'wrote these things down ... we know his testimony is true' (21:24).

Who was he? With one voice, early church leaders said 'John, the son of Zebedee'. Their thinking was partly deductive (if BD is not John, wherever has John got to?) and partly traditional (accounts known to them but lost to us). We call this the *external evidence* (facts from outside the Bible). It is quoted by Irenaeus, Eusebius, Tertullian, Clement and Origen. All of them (needless to say) were far closer to the events than anyone who has disputed the evidence. Their insistence is all the more impressive since the Fourth Gospel went through a period of unpopularity because it became a happy hunting-ground (quoted grossly out of context) for second-century 'Gnostic' heretics.[8]

The *internal evidence* (facts from inside the Bible) is impressive too. Pursuing a Sherlock Holmes-like policy of deduction by elimination, scholars from the nineteenth-century Bishop Westcott onwards have developed an argument in ever-narrowing circles. Comparing scores of linguistic

---

8. Authorship of the Fourth Gospel in early tradition: See Smalley, chapter 2, 'Who Was John?' and Milne, Introduction.

shades of meaning, geographical references, and Gospel cross-references that explain or complement one another, they have reasoned like this. The writer was a Jew. He was a Palestinian Jew. He knew Jerusalem intimately before it was destroyed in AD 70. He was familiar with cross-currents of thought in Jerusalem around 30-40. He was a disciple of Jesus. He was one of 'the twelve'. He was one of the inner circle within the twelve (Peter, James and John). And finally (with a flourish) *he was John.*

It is impressive. I find it as convincing as anything could be, in the absence of a clear naming of the writer by himself. Why did he not name himself? One has to assume it was out of modesty.

Against all of this, 'modern' scholars have strenuously denied John's authorship. Some of the objections are to do with chronology and some with style, and to these I shall return. Surely the most fatuous is the objection that one of two brethren called 'sons of thunder' because of their short fuses could not have become the theologian who specialises in *love* (compare Mark 3:17 and 9:38 with Luke 9:54 and then, in contrast, John 15:12-17 and 1 John 3:11). It is an odd idea. *Someone* was sufficiently wrought upon by the grace of God as to see his character slowly transformed into one of self-giving love. Why not John, who kept such close company with Love Personified?

The objections also fail to reckon on the implications (or even the possibility) of *divine inspiration.* To that we must return later.

Questions deserving an answer

All of this, fascinating as it is to explore, does underline that there are 'difficulties' in the Fourth Gospel. For all its depth and beauty, this Gospel raises questions. Why is it so different from the others? Are the words conveyed as from the lips of Jesus really his, or the unknown author's? Did the incidents described really happen, and why does the writer almost invariably portray scenes apparently unknown to the other three?

To these questions I want to return in the next chapter. The devout Christian need not fear them. John (we shall see) is faithful to his oft-repeated wish to be a *witness to truth*. Those who knew him best towards the end of his life, and who added their own testimony, were sure of that: 'This is the disciple who testifies to these things, and who wrote them down. We know that his testimony is true' (21:24).

Chapter 14

GOOD NEWS WITH A DIFFERENCE

The Fourth Gospel is *different*. People approaching it for the first time often sense this, without being able to explain the feeling. This applies, whether the newly-arrived reader has already learned something of the previous three, or whether all he has is a kind of subliminal folk-memory of the Christmas story, the Sermon on the Mount, the 'golden rule', and the parable of the Prodigal Son ... and feels that this is somehow on a different plane.

As I began to write this chapter, a thoughtful young Christian man, skilled in computer technology, said to me, 'I've just read John's Gospel right through, and was astonished to see how different it is from the others. It has the feel of a different kind of book altogether. I even had an odd sense that it described a different Jesus!'

He quickly qualified the comment, for he understands the truth of the matter. But his remark would have pleased some of the scholars and theologians who have tried for over a century now to discredit John's Gospel as a truthful and apostolic account. Presenting it as a kind of cross between *Pilgrim's Progress* and *Ben Hur*, they have praised its spiritual symbolism but doubted its literal connection with anything actually said or done by Jesus of Nazareth.

The wilder extremes of critical speculation have denied that the book is main-line Christian at all. Pushing it into the second century, they have identified it as an expression of Christianized 'Gnosticism', that amorphous movement which by then was becoming such a threat to the Church, with its

seductive offers of 'secret knowledge' as the true way of salvation.[1] The writer (whoever he was) is conceived as putting
into the mouth of Jesus his own developing mysticism, and
then using some creative imagination (to put it mildly) to
produce miracle-signed 'settings' for the teaching.

To be fair to the critics, this is exactly what some of the
Gnostic 'Gospels' did in fact attempt. The so-called 'Gospel
of Thomas' is the best-known example.

But the Jesus of these pious fictions is a shadowy, shapeless figure lacking both personality and activity, who sits
around, Socrates-like, uttering complicated aphorisms a good
deal less clear than those of that philosopher! In contrast, the
Jesus of John's Gospel is precisely that powerful, personable
figure who has gripped the attention and captured the loyalty
of millions from the time it was written to this day. As Roy
Clements said: '...the person you discover [in the Fourth Gos-
pel] is not only more human than the synoptic newsreels
might convey, he is also much more divine; he is not only
easier to love, he is also more compelling to worship.'[2]

Spot the differences
I recall from childhood those clever double-pictures in com-
ics and magazines that appear at first glance to be exactly
alike, but in fact include about twenty differences which the
contestant must spot. Try this with John and the Synopists.

---

1. *Gnosis* means 'knowledge'. Gnosticism was not an organised movement but an amorphous trend of thinking that threw up many movements. Some elements of modern 'New Age' thinking are analogous.
Gnostics set the material and spiritual worlds in hostile contrast. Their
concept of salvation had little to do with morality or forgiveness; it
was sought by an ascent through levels of spiritual awareness through
the gaining of secret knowledge. In the New Testament, both John and
Paul may be warning against very early attempts at gnostic thinking.
See 1 John 1:1-4; 2:18-27; 4:1-3; Colossians 2:1-10; 1 Timothy 6:20-21 (the
opposing ideas of what is falsely called knowledge).
2. Roy Clements, *Introducing Jesus*, p. 13.

You will find the differences surprising and slightly perplexing. But they need no help from the Gnostics (or the more bizarre Bible-critics) to find their explanation.

John writes differently

His style is meditative, elliptical, full of abstract concept-words; Light, Life, Love, Glory, Only-begotten, Eternal Life, and so on. He begins his story, not with a brief account of Jesus' birth or early ministry, but with that soaring prologue that takes us back into another world and a past eternity.

John presents his material differently

He is drastically and unashamedly selective and admits as much.

> Jesus did many other miraculous signs ... which are not recorded in this book. But *these* are written that you may believe (John 20: 30-31, emphasis mine).

As a consequence, he leaves strange gaps in the story. The basic facts are so well known to established Christians that this can fail to register. But the remarkable fact is that John *makes no mention* of Jesus' birth or baptism, his temptations, his Sermon on the Mount, his casting out of demons, or his healing of lepers. From John we learn nothing of Christ's turning-point challenge, 'Who do you say that I am?'; nothing of the 'transfiguration', and nothing of the agony in Gethsemane. The only miracle undoubtedly paralleled from the other accounts is the feeding of the five thousand (and the lake scene that followed).

In other words, if we had only John's account to go by, we would know nothing of most of the outstanding features in Jesus' life and ministry!

John's geography is different

The three Synoptic Gospels have based the ministry of Jesus in lakeside Galilee. They hint of wider travels north and east, and then tell of the final southern confrontation in Jerusalem. In striking contrast, John describes only two lakeland incidents, but pictures Jesus making regular visits to the capital, especially for the great successive religious feasts. Here is what can only be described as an unsuspected Judaean ministry.

John employs a different time-scale

Without actually saying so, the Synoptists can easily give the impression of a public ministry lasting only one year. The whole story *could* be compressed into a mere twelve-month period, and only one annual Passover is mentioned (the feast at which Christ died). In contrast, John mentions at least two previous Passovers, and requires three to four years to cover the events.

So far the contrasts are interesting, even curious, but no more. They certainly present no fundamental problem. The traditional explanation has been that John, in later years, deliberately filled in some of the gaps in the Synoptic record that understandably focused on Galilee (after all, seven of the apostles were Galileans). But here now is a real problem.

The figure of Jesus himself is disconcertingly different

He makes larger claims for himself. 'Son of Man' is replaced (in most cases) by 'Only Son of God'. Deeply metaphysical explanations are given of the relationship between Father and Son. He even makes the astounding statement that seeing him means seeing God.[3]

He teaches in a different manner. Gone are the simple parables with their one-lesson punch-lines. Gone are the terse aphorisms and earthy analogies. Instead we hear elaborate

---

3. The claims of Jesus in John's Gospel: 5:16-30; 6:35-40; 8: 27-30; 14: 1-14.

allegories in which every point and detail has its real-life counterpart. Instead of a shepherd who seeks one straying sheep, we have a sheep-pen, a gate, a robber, a watchman, a stranger, a wolf, and of course, the sheep and the shepherd; each with their spiritual equivalents (see John 10).

Christ's way of speaking is less graphic and colloquial; more formal, abstract, doctrinal, almost mystical. The thought-forms and concepts that he handles seem to have changed subtly. He introduces what has been called a 'modified dualism'; a repeated contrast between light and darkness, life and death, truth and error.[4] It has been estimated that John has about 150 important words on the lips of Jesus that are never used by the other Gospel writers.

And he talks about different things! The kingdom of God (that central theme of the Synoptics), is almost absent ... now the theme is *salvation*, or *eternal life*. People are not so much called to follow the inaugurator of God's kingdom: rather they are urged to have faith in the person of God's Son.

Theological flights of fancy

Not surprisingly, radical critics of the New Testament have had a field-day with the Fourth Gospel. For example, the 'History of Religions' school of thought dislikes any idea of divine revelation, preferring to see mankind as struggling upwards to ever higher forms of religion, borrowing freely from different cultures as they go along.

Their argument from the Fourth Gospel goes something like this. Palestinian Jews in the time of Jesus simply did not talk or think the way Jesus is reported to speak in this Gos-

---

4. Dualism sees good and evil, light and darkness, 'God' and Satan as equal-and-opposite, locked in never-ending conflict. The Christian Gospel (and the Jewish Faith) recognises the reality of the conflict, but sees evil as a distortion of good, not as an absolute reality. Satan will be defeated. This emphasis could be called a 'modified dualism'; although it is not classic dualism at all.

pel. On the other hand, Asian Gnostics a century later did. 'John', they suggest, was some anonymous second-century theologian leading a network of Asian churches, who has produced an impressive piece of theological reflection on the meaning (to him) of Jesus of Nazareth. The simple story of the Palestinian prophet has evolved into the God-Man Redeemer, incarnate and then glorified. But any factual link between the two is minimal. The Fourth Gospel (they say) is impressive spirituality clothed in pious fiction.[5]

Of course this is completely unacceptable to the Bible-believing Christian. The Church has been from the beginning aware of 'problems' with the Fourth Gospel, but has resolved them by making four points. First, John devoted his attention to those very facts only lightly touched on by the earlier writers. Second, he has deliberately introduced more interpretation and reflection. Thirdly, his account echoes Christ's ministry as it was carried out in a different context (sophisticated, argumentative and reflective Jerusalem, rather than unsophisticated rural, action-orientated Galilee). Fourthly, John was writing rather later than the others, and to an Asian readership very different from the Roman or Palestinian readership of the synoptic Gospels. To help his readership through new and different situations and enable them to resist new and different religious challenges, he naturally

---

5. Early this century Rudolf Bultmann was one of those who popularised the notion that John's ideas were drawn from a 'pre-Christian Mandean myth' connected with the roots of Persian religion. Oddly enough the modern Mandean sect in Iraq and Iran has a 'Book of John' amongst its sayings-collections. However there is no evidence whatever of such teaching as early as the first century AD, and any resemblance to John's writings is purely one of a few word-similarities. Other less radical reconstructions have tried to connect John with some of the 'Gnostic Gospels', but the dating really does not work. John was not 'christianising' the Gnostics, rather some of them were trying to 'gnosticise' John! See Smalley *John – Evangelist* and *Interpreter*, chapter 2 and Carson, pp. 29-33.

draws out the incidents and the teachings that are most relevant to the changed situation.

None of that threatens belief in a God-inspired writing. Rather, it bears witness to such divine aid. None of it casts doubt on the truth of the words and deeds of Jesus recorded here. Rather, it testifies to the One who was the ideal communicator.

The new look
Much of this is now acknowledged by theologians and scholars. For the last thirty years the 'New Look of Johannine Studies' has gathered momentum. Let me list some of the factors in this new thinking, which in many ways confirm the faith of those Christians who always remained unshaken in their devotion to John's Gospel as part of God's own witness to his Son.[6]

The discovery of the famous Qumran Scrolls shortly after the Second World War caused severe re-thinking. For here was another collection of religious documents dating from the very same time and place as John's account of Jesus' ministry. And there are dramatic resemblances. The Qumran Community Rule, for example, speaks of 'practising truth'. It contrasts 'children of light and children of darkness'. It presents 'the knowledge of God' as the way to life. It reflects precisely that 'modified dualism' between truth and lies, light and darkness, good and evil, which we have seen permeating the Fourth Gospel.

Of course, Qumran does not present the Christian gospel. For the earnest Dead Sea Community, eternal life was found (they hoped) in meticulous obedience to God's Law, whereas for John it is found through faith in God's Son. But the concepts are similar, the presupposed problem is the same, the language is parallel.

---

6. For a detailed treatment of the 'New Look', see Smalley, chapter 1, and (in even more detail) Carson, *The Gospel According to John* in his 103 page 'Introduction'.

In other words what Qumran shows is that Jesus' language (i.e. the Fourth Gospel) is not that of second-century Asia, but of first-century Palestine. John reports it precisely because Jesus used it. Jesus used it because it was the religious language of Jerusalem and Judaea, and he knew himself to be the fulfilment of all its hopes and longings.

Digging up the evidence

Archaeology now steps in. John's references to places in Jerusalem and Judaea (once cheerfully assumed to be as non-literal and symbolic as places in John Bunyan's *Holy War*) are now known to be accurate and meaningful. I have heard Israeli archaeologists half-jokingly describe the Fourth Gospel as a guidebook to the holy city in the time of Jesus.

I mentioned earlier the Pools of Bethesda where Jesus healed the lame man (see page 23). Another Pool is that of Siloam. To this place Jesus sent a blind man to wash and receive his sight. John makes a little aside, *siloam* means 'sent' (John 9:1-12). Like the five porches of Bethesda, this has been read as a piece of spiritualizing symbolism. But the explorations of a Victorian English soldier revealed a literal paved pool at the receiving end of a remarkable tunnel that piped water through the hillside from the city's only natural water supply, the Gihon Spring. King Hezekiah, in the time of the prophet Isaiah, had commissioned the tunnel (which now bears his name). He had literally 'sent' the water safely inside the city, as a defence against war and siege.

Solomon's portico provides another example. John pictures Jesus walking and teaching there during the winter festival of Hanukkah (Dedication). After Pentecost it apparently became a regular meeting place for the early church (John 10:22-24; Acts 3:11; 5:12). Although now replaced by the Muslim pavement surrounding the Dome of the Rock and the El Aksah Mosque, its location has been calculated and is often shown on archaeological reconstructions, models and

maps of Herod's Temple. It was in fact the eastern boundary
of the temple courtyard (directly opposite the better-known
'wailing' or 'western' wall). It faced across the Kidron Valley (also mentioned by John) towards the Mount of Olives.
Because the eastern slope is precipitous, Herod was not able
to extend that side with retaining walls, as he did the other
three boundaries. So, although that crafty king did reconstruct the line with great stone pillars (creating the portico
effect), the more spiritual rabbis, uneasy about the King's
mixed motives and bloodstained record, were able to reas-
sure people that this was still part of Solomon's original temple (hence the name) and insisted on doing their teaching
only there.

As Professor A. M. Hunter, one of the pioneers of the 'New
Look' has emphasized, these two simple verses of John get it
exactly right, and bear all the imprint of personal recollection.[7]

Then came the Feast of Dedication at Jerusalem. It was
winter, and Jesus was in the temple area walking in Solomon's Colonnade (10:22-23).

The Feast was (and is) indeed a winter festival. Nestled
west of Olivet, roofed and shielded by its own wall, the colonnade made winter open-air preaching possible in reason-
able comfort. With retrospective knowledge, we can reflect
on the poignancy of the scene. The entry to the porches was
through the Eastern or Golden Gate, which stood directly
opposite the great Altar of Burnt Offering once the portico
was crossed. This gateway must have been that entered by
Jesus on Palm Sunday. Beside the route lay the Garden of
Gethsemane.[8]

A third example must suffice. John (alone) mentions a

---

7. A. M. Hunter, *According to John*, chapter 2.
8. Eastern ('Golden') Gate: Ezekiel 11:1; 43:1-5; 46:1-3; Luke 19:28-
48; 22:39-46; John 18:1-14.

platform or raised pavement called Gabbatha (the Stone Pavement). On this the governor Pilate sat to pronounce sentence on the imprisoned Jesus (19:12-16). Pilate seems to have constantly appeared and re-appeared here, as he alternated between public arguments with the Jewish accusers and private interviews with the divine prisoner (as chapters 18 and 19 relate). Scholars are not quite unanimous about this location, but most agree that the long-venerated Catholic and Orthodox site beside the traditional Via Dolorosa is in fact the place. Here are massive stone blocks and a Roman roadway 'rippled' to carry chariot wheels (plus evidence of games played by bored Roman soldiers).[9]

Enough has been said. Scholar after scholar (including many who have no dogmatic interest in 'proving' the Fourth Gospel) acknowledges that the 'tradition drawn on by the evangelist' betrays an intimate knowledge of Jerusalem during the ministry of Jesus. When we read these words, we are hearing echoes of an 'original source'.

Reaching a verdict

We could continue, but space forbids. Let me sum up the state of the case. Once we rid our minds of the fantasy of a writer who never knew Jesus or Jerusalem producing a well-meaning but basically untrue piece of piety, we see how comparatively easily the notorious 'differences' are resolved.

John writes differently, for he has reflected on the issues for half a lifetime. He writes selectively for the reason that he confesses. He makes no mention of many of the major

---

9. See my *Living In the Promised Land*, chapter 8, 'With God in the Garden'. The *Dictionary of Jesus and the Gospels* suggests a site for Gabbatha on the cliff-face still visible immediately west of the Wailing Wall. Earlier archaeologists favoured the area of Herod's palace, where 'the Citadel' stands today (opposite Christ Church). Whatever the precise location, references outside of the Bible make it clear that the Pavement existed, was well known, and 'fits' John's account of the trial. See Smalley, page 36.

events, because they are already widely known (although in fact he refers to them obliquely, as I shall show). His geography is different precisely because he relates the Jerusalem ministry rather than the Galilee-phase.

He employs a different time-scale simply because the intermittent ministry in the south lasted longer than the more concentrated ministry in the north. (In fact there is a remarkable inter-relation between the timing of John and the Synoptics. While it is impossible to condense the Johannine calendar into the Synoptists' timetable, the reverse process is quite easy: Mark's story can be expanded within John's, and each casts light on the other.)

What of the more profound differences? Why does Jesus 'sound' different in the Fourth Gospel? I make two suggestions.

First, because the Son of God was a powerful communicator (was, indeed, God's Communication, as the word *logos* implies, 1:1-5). When he ministered in Jerusalem, the centre of sophisticated theology, he adopted that kind of language. It was a medium which, as the Dead Sea Scrolls now indicate, set Jerusalem and Judaea alight with excitement and debate.

There is nothing strange or inconsistent about this. Let me, without immodesty I hope, give a personal illustration. I am called to preach the gospel and to teach the Bible. A typical month may find me addressing in turn a children's school assembly, a Free Church congregation, an enquirers' class of new converts (or people not yet converted), a dinner which suspicious non-Christians have been persuaded by their churchgoing friends to attend, and a debate conducted by a secular club for retired professional men. In slightly more youthful days, I could well add examples of a ten-minute talk at a Yorkshire sheep-auction, a lunchtime meeting at a Glasgow shipyard gate, a discussion in the Members' Dining Room of the House of Commons, a soup-kitchen meeting for Chicago homeless, a Texas radio phone-in, a debate on the Resurrection in a New York lawyers' training school, and a conducted tour of the Garden Tomb in Jerusalem for professors from the Hebrew University! Each of these opportunities for Christian witness had to be conducted in a style appropriate to the audience. The basic message was essentially the same in each case. But the difference in approach appropriate (for example) to the Chicago homeless and the Israeli academics was almost total.

Of course, Jesus communicated in one style with the Jerusalem authorities and in another with Galilean farmers. What is mysterious about that? One of the Saviour's greatest advocates, the apostle Paul, addressed Athenian philosophers and Jewish synagogue attenders in almost completely different terms – compare Acts 13:13-43 with Acts 17:16-34. This is the challenge today of cross-cultural evangelism.

My second point about Jesus' 'style' is this. We often think of his brisk sayings and pointed parables (as recorded by the Synoptists) as the original and then wonder uneasily whether John was justified in 'expanding' them. But what if John accurately reflects the original teaching, and the other three writers condense it? For example, must we think of the allegory of the Good Shepherd as an elaborate extension of the Parable of the Lost Sheep in Luke 15? Why should the parable not rather be a condensation of the allegory (condensed either by Jesus himself on a different occasion, or by Luke for his Greek readers)?

The situation would then be that Luke gives 'the truth and nothing but the truth', whereas John gives 'the whole truth'! John's version of Jesus' teaching then becomes analogous to his version of the chronology. In both cases, we do not have to squeeze John into the Synoptists – we fit the Synoptists neatly into John.

This is a view favoured increasingly by modern scholars. It finds support in the attitude of early Church teachers (who, after all, were far closer to the events!). When Tatian wrote his 'Four-In-One Gospel' (see page 21) this was his assumption. He took John's Gospel as the basic framework and built the other material into it. So, for example, he began with John's 'Prologue' and followed it with Luke's and Matthew's 'Christmas Stories'. He made Jesus' visits to the Jerusalem Feasts his time-frame, and fitted into it the Galilee Ministry and the Journey to Jerusalem.

This has been a lengthy parenthesis in our examination of the Fourth Gospel, but I hope it has been worthwhile. We need have no doubt. In John's writing we hear the authentic voice of Jesus. He said:

'I tell you the truth, whoever hears my word and believes him who sent me has eternal life and will not be condemned; he has crossed over from death to life' (5:24).

It matters as much as that.

Chapter 15

JOHN'S DIVINE DRAMA

It may startle some Christians to see the sublime Fourth Gospel described as a *drama*. But I want to suggest that one way to explore some of the riches is to view it as superb theatre.

I don't imply, of course, that it was intended to be a play performed on stage. But many scholars have pointed out how full it is of 'dramatic narrative' and how powerfully the writer deploys the skills of the dramatist to fulfil that request first made by Greek visitors to Jerusalem, 'Sir, we would like to see Jesus' (12:21).

Dorothy Sayers well understood this, and she relied on John even more than on Matthew for the inspiration and the material of her play-cycle *The Man Born to Be King*. No less than five of her episodes were virtually paraphrases and reconstructions of chapters from the Fourth Gospel: 'A Certain Nobleman', 'Bread of Heaven', 'The Feast of Tabernacles', 'The Light and the Life', and 'The Princes of This World'. The very titles sound familiar to any lover of John's Gospel!

With consummate skill, John musters several dramatic techniques. A close examination can be fascinating: join me in one.

1. Both sides of the curtain

The narrative often operates at two levels at once. The writer is deliberately ambiguous about which level he implies. One example often commented on is the phrase 'lifted up'. In a scene full of high drama and pathos, Jesus says 'But I, when

I am lifted up from the earth, will draw all men to myself'
(12:32-33). John adds the comment that Jesus was referring
to his death on the cross, when in the most grim and literal
way he was indeed lifted up. But there is a double meaning.
For the 'drawing of all' did not literally happen at Calvary;
rather Christ's death opened the way for multitudes through
the ages to be attracted to their Saviour. But the 'lifting up'
has more than one meaning too. The inspired writer is uplifting Christ by his very exercise of writing – that is indeed his
declared purpose. Furthermore, he is promising that whenever the Church proclaims the crucified Saviour, people will
be drawn to him. The modern song *Lift Jesus Higher* is not
the irritating misuse of biblical words that some of its critics
think! It catches something of John's inspired comment!

The two-level emphasis is present at the beginning and
the end. When the first disciples hesitantly ask Jesus where
he is staying, there is more to it than an enquiry about bed-
and-breakfast. They wonder where he is 'from' in the deepest sense. After all, he has just been pointed out as the Lamb
of God (1:29, 35-42).

In similar vein at the end, Pilate also asks where he is
from (19:9). Luke has told us how the literal answer ('from
Galilee') provided the governor with a half-chance of dodging responsibility. But behind and beneath that, Pilate was
worried about the Prisoner's origin. That perplexing figure
had already hinted at this. 'My kingdom is not of this world.
... my kingdom is from another place. ... for this I came into
the world, to testify to the truth' (18:36-37).[1]

---

1. I owe this insight to Smalley's 'Drama in the Fourth Gospel', part of
chapter 6 in his *Jesus – Evangelist and Interpreter*. He writes, 'John's
thought always operates on two levels at once ... such is his deliberate
ambivalence that we are never quite sure at any one moment on which level
he is to be understood – the earthly or the heavenly, in time or in eternity ...
John has two theatres in mind at once' pp. 192-193.

2. The power of irony

Drama often depends on irony or even satire. The audience, 'told' more than the characters in the play, smile, wince and groan or chuckle at the ironic misunderstandings or mis-statements in the story. There is a very high level of such dry comment in the Fourth Gospel. It comes out most obviously in the exchanges between Jesus, the hostile religious authorities, and the temple crowds milling halfway between the two.

For example, at the Feast of Tabernacles the crowd argue about Jesus' antecedents. 'He is the Christ', say some. Others object, 'How can the Christ come from Galilee? – Bethlehem is Messiah's home.' John records this tongue-in-cheek: he and his readers know that although Jesus came from Galilee, he was born in Bethlehem. A few hours later the temple guards return empty-handed after being told to arrest the Preacher. A bitter argument breaks out in the Sanhedrin. This time the objection is that 'none of the rulers or Pharisees believe in him'. But in fact one does ... Nicodemus, who took the 'lead part' in an earlier scene, makes at least a cautious half-confession. 'John grins to himself' (as Bruce Milne suggests) and the audience chuckle with him. Meanwhile, flushed and angry, the other members of the council make the same fatuous mistake about Galilee and Bethlehem (7:40-52).[2]

The irony reaches a climax in the trial scenes. The reader can see that the Prisoner is really the judge, and all of the other characters are 'on trial': Judas the betrayer, Peter the denier, the Jewish accusers, and most obviously of all Pilate the judge. At points this is almost unbearable in its tension. The audience want to cry out – 'Can't you *see*?'

The religious leaders are scrupulous about ceremonial uncleanness whilst utterly unscrupulous in their twisting of

---

2. Milne, *The Message of John* pp. 121-122. This writer frequently underlines the ironic twists, with phrases like 'tongue in cheek', 'John is grinning again', 'John again has his tongue in his cheek'.

morality and justice. Pilate asks 'What is truth?' but is sup-
pressing the obvious truth that Jesus is innocent. Pilate utters the words (glorious to Christian ears), *'Ecce Homo*, Behold the man' (John 19:5, AV), but all he thinks he means is
'Here is the person all this struggle is about'. He threatens
Jesus with power over his life, yet is powerless to do what
conscience and facts demand. 'Here is your king,' he says in
bitter mockery to the Jews ... and never said a truer word!

To add to all of this dramatic potential, the whole of this
(chapters 18 and 19) take place literally on two stages. The
governor's public arguments with the Jewish authorities are
constantly interrupted by private conversations with the Prisoner. (Dorothy Sayers imagined the alternating scenes with
only a curtain between, so that in the background to the private interviews there could be heard the murmuring and mut-
tering of the crowd.) Here, in heightened form, is John's other
device of 'two scenes, two meanings, two worlds'.

3. Dramatic construction

Drama, of course, depends on character displayed under pressure, on the tension between competing interests, and on the
dialogue coupled with action that is produced by this. Obviously the action and dialogue need to take place fairly
statically – in the drawing room, beside the market cross, in
the solicitor's office, etc. John has numerous 'scenes' which
exactly fulfil these criteria. Some of them involve just two
characters; those interviews, as I have already called them.
We watch Jesus and Nathanael, Jesus and Nicodemus, Jesus
and the Samaritan woman, Jesus and Peter by the lake.

The tension is built up by developing dialogue (often with
those ironic asides). Chapter 4 provides a classic example.
Jesus is thirsty, and asks a woman for water from her bucket
at the well-side. Her cheeky response underlines how surprising this is (no Jewish rabbi would speak to a woman alone
... no respectable Jew would share a drinking vessel with a

Samaritan). Irony immediately appears; Jesus can offer 'living water' (although he is thirsty!)

The woman ignorantly or knowingly misunderstands, and Jesus speaks more clearly of 'water welling up to eternal life'. The woman (now understanding) jumps at the offer. But first she must be brought to face her own moral condition. Jesus' request to meet her husband pinpoints this. Her evasive reply is swiftly challenged with gentle but steely irony; 'You are right when you say you have no husband – you've had five, and the sixth time you haven't bothered to marry!'

The woman now neatly changes the subject, in order to avoid the challenge (her evasion is one which we are all familiar with, when we engage in personal witnessing ... 'There are so many different churches; how can I tell which one is right?'). But there can be no dodging; Jesus utters one of his absolutes about the true God and true worship. A further attempt at evasion ('Let's leave these profound subjects to the promised Messiah') only opens the door to Jesus' self-revelation ...'I am the Messiah'. The woman's conversion is complete, and she bears immediate witness, as two other groups come on-stage – the disciples and the villagers.

This is high drama, skilfully deployed. That does not imply that John has been 'creative' (imaginative) in his account. The scene actually happened, I firmly believe. But John highlights what happened, with dramatic skill.

There is much more. John also develops highly complex 'Acts' made up of several brief 'Scenes', each involving two individuals, or one person and one group, usually in tension with one another. The masterly tale of the healing of the blind man (chapter 9) offers a splendid example, full of characterisation, satire and gentle fun.

Scene 1: Jesus and his disciples (1-5)
Scene 2: Jesus and the blind man (6-7)
Scene 3: The healed man and his neighbours (8-12)
Scene 4: The religious leaders and the healed man (13-17)
Scene 5: The religious leaders and his parents (18-23)
Scene 6: The religious leaders and the man (again) (24-34)
Scene 7: Jesus and the man (35-38)
Scene 8: Jesus and the religious leaders (39-41)

The hostile authorities become increasingly flustered: the pert character who causes all the fuss becomes increasingly sure that Jesus is someone very special.

Throughout the Act there is tension, irony, superb humour, and something going on at two levels. There are high points (at which, in a real theatre the curtain would drop, and the audience would react with gasps or a buzz of comment). And there are sublime truths expressed – sometimes directly and openly, sometimes by implication:

'While I am in the world, I am the light of the world.'
'I went and washed and then I could see.'
'Ask him, he is of age, he will speak for himself.'
'One thing I do know, I was blind but now I see.'
'Do you believe ...?' 'Lord I believe.'
'For judgment I have come into this world.'

4. Visual aids and props

On the stage some scenery is required; the 'props' of the theatre. They should not be elaborate, for their purpose is not to draw attention to themselves, but to focus and heighten the dialogue. They are assistants to the spoken word, not its rivals.

In the Gospel, of course, the stage props are verbal too. They gain their 'visual' impact from suggestion and atmosphere. The writer uses two devices; the *signs* and the *feasts*.

First, look at the signs. This is the name (*semeia*) which John uniquely gives to Christ's miracles. They are designed not so much to draw attention to the power of the kingdom or the compassion of the Master (like those in the Synoptic Gospels). Rather they point to the truth that Jesus wants to convey.

With some (like the first, the Wedding at Cana, 2:11) the reader is left to see the point unaided. The waterpots designed for ritual purification provide the clue. Jesus turns the cold water of religious legalism into the joyful wine of gospel assurance. William Temple commented, 'the modest water saw its God and blushed'.[3]

Some signs are followed by one of the striking 'I AM' sayings (more of this later). After restoring sight to the blind man Jesus announces, 'I am the light of the world' (9:5). Other signs are followed by a lengthy 'Discourse' (either a sermon by Jesus or a lively debate with friends and foes).

My point is this: the miracles so vividly described, provide a 'visual aid' to the truths expressed. They offer a mental backdrop to the dramatic dialogues. We gasp with the onlookers, as Jesus commands the stone to be rolled from Lazarus' tomb.[4] We see the charcoal fire burning on the shore, lit by Jesus himself, not from gathered driftwood but with material carried there. The last time a charcoal fire burned, it was in the courtyard of the high priest's palace, and beside it Peter denied his Master three times. Now he will be given three opportunities to affirm his love. This whole scene of almost unbearable poignancy is choreographed by Jesus himself, to recall not only the denial, but the original call to apostleship after a fruitless night of fishing. The message signalled with overwhelming force is 'This same Jesus is

---

3. William Temple, *Reading in John's Gospel*, p. 36.
4. John 11:38-44. Notice how many successive 'scenes' lead up to the enormous climax: Lazarus and his sisters (1-3), Jesus and his disciples (4-16), Jesus and Martha (17-27), Jesus and Mary (28-37) and Jesus at the tomb (38-44).

still with you, after death and resurrection – still calling you
to evangelism and pastoral care – catch human fish, and feed
human sheep, confident of the abiding presence of the Living Christ'.[5]

Festivals and ceremonies

Another 'verbal visual aid' (if I may coin the phrase) is presented by the theme of *festival* that constantly occurs in John's
book. As I mentioned earlier, the Fourth Gospel reveals the
hitherto unsuspected fact that Jesus frequently travelled south
from Galilee, to visit the capital city at those times when the
great Feasts and Fasts drew thousands to Jerusalem. Almost
at the start, he attends the greatest feast of all (Passover) and
creates a sensation by his 'Cleansing of the Temple' (2:12-
25).[6] Nor was this a brief appearance. 'While he was in Jerusalem at the Passover Feast, many people saw the miraculous signs he was doing, and believed in his name' (2:23).
When a leading Pharisee surreptitiously visited him, the re-
nown of his 'signs' was already effective (3:1-2). The visits
are repeated; another Passover implied (6:1-4), then the Feast
of Tabernacles, to which a very long section of public debate
and controversy is devoted (chapters 7-9). Then came 'the
Feast of Dedication' (10:22) where his winter preaching took
place so appropriately. Finally we have the events of Passion
Week built around the successive feasts of Unleavened Bread
(Preparation) and Passover.

On these great public occasions, Jesus turned the colourful festivals into visual aids to his own ministry. 'Tabernac-

---

5. Luke 5:1-11; John 18:18-27; 21:1-25.
6. I leave untouched here the vexed question as to whether there were
two demonstrations in the temple, one at the start of Christ's ministry
(as John implies, and which I include in my suggested chronology
found in the Appendix) and another at the end (as the Synoptists described) ... or whether John uses dramatic and artistic licence to 'move'
the event forward. It is worth commenting that Josephus records at
least four attempts to remove the abuses of the temple merchants.

les' recalled the travels of the people of Israel through the Sinai Desert after their escape from captivity. Ceremonies reflected incidents during that period; the water that broke from the rock at Moses' command, the manna that fed the hungry people, the light of the 'pillar of fire' that guided the pilgrims. So the temple courts were kept ablaze with torches, and water was carried up the slope from Siloam Pool to be poured before the altar. It was against this background, with enormous significance, that Jesus announced himself as the Light of the World, and 'on the last and greatest day of the Feast ... stood up and said in a loud voice, If anyone is thirsty, let him come to me and drink'.[7]

'The language is simple; the claim is august'.[8] All that the sacred biblical history recalls and promises is fulfilled in this lonely figure who 'stands and calls out' at critical moments in the celebrations. It takes little imagination for the reader to 'see' this vivid backcloth to the claims of Christ.

Enough has been said. I don't want to labour the point. All of the Four Gospels have been classified as 'dramatic narratives', but none is so dramatic as John. Before and behind the curtain, with irony and double meaning, through short 'scenes' and elaborate 'acts', with dialogue and discourse, aided by near-visible signs and festivals, he presents the powerful drama of the Son of God from Heaven, the Word made flesh, the Lamb of God bearing away the sin of the world.

Truly, John's Gospel soars like an eagle.

---

7. Feast of Tabernacles: Exodus 16 and 17; John 7:1-5, 14-24, 37-44.
8. Milne, p. 119.

Chapter 16

A PATTERN OF TRUTH

The man's face on the television screen brought back a string of memories. Ten years ago he attended most of a series of sermons that I preached in a small English church, based on the early chapters of John's Gospel. A thoughtful and sensitive man, he was groping his way from a nominal and conventional Christian profession towards a more personal commitment. His two hesitations were intellectual and moral: did it make sense to 'believe' in today's situation? And could he get rid of his sense of guilt? By the end of the series, he was able to answer a resounding 'yes' to both questions.

It was a reminder to me, as I switched off the TV news and began to write this chapter; a reminder of the principal purpose that John had in mind as he wrote his Gospel. Bringing people to faith in Christ, the Son of God, that was his chief concern, as he freely confessed. To that end he selected and set out his material.

No statistics are available, but anecdotal evidence (as they call it) gives the overwhelming impression that more people have found God through the Fourth Gospel than through the other three put together. Certainly the evangelical preacher will find it to be one of his most powerful weapons in the battle to win the hearts and souls of people. I have 'preached through John' in each of my pastorates, as well as repeating some of the process again in shorter series, like 'John's picture of Love', 'Truth from the Upper Room', 'People Jesus met', and so on.

I don't keep all of my 'used sermon notes' but I do have several hundred filed. I notice with interest that I have preached (at least) 40 sermons from Mark, 70 from Matthew, 90 from Luke and 130 from John. This is not surprising: this Gospel presents material that begs to be preached. More than that: it is preaching in print!

Many scholars have noticed this and drawn their conclusions. Some suggest that what we have as the finished product is the memory of the Ephesian Church's experience of John's preaching (very much as Mark reports Peter's preaching). 'Think of the material in John's Gospel as first of all sermonic', says Donald Carson in his recent scholarly and evangelical commentary.[1]

This involves two things. First, much of the material is in fact a record of the way Jesus himself preached. Secondly, John selects and presents the material as 'proclamation'. This (it seems to me) best accounts for the sometimes strange omissions and inclusions (compared with the other three Evangelists). 'The fourth Evangelist is interested in presenting certain truths to certain people, and he exercises the preacher's prerogative of shaping his message accordingly'.[2]

Does this mean that John underlined his points by elaborating on Jesus' words or putting expressions into the Saviour's mouth? I don't believe so. If we follow some of the more 'liberal' critics (who think he did exactly that) we would reach the bizarre conclusion that John saw more deeply, preached more powerfully and communicated more effectively than Jesus himself! But John sets the material in a certain order, and then adds his own little 'asides' (directed by the Spirit of God) so that we can 'hear' that Prince of Preachers, the Son of God, all the more clearly. Look at some examples, which are eloquent in their significance.

After the turning of water into wine, John comments: 'This

1. D. A. Carson, *The Gospel According to John.* See especially pp. 45-49.
2. *ibid*, p. 47.

first sign Jesus performed at Cana ... and thus revealed his glory.'

After the miracles at Passover time: 'Many "believed" in his name, but Jesus would not entrust himself to them ... he knew what was in a man' (AV).

After Christ's meeting with the woman at the well: 'Many of the Samaritans from that town believed in him because of the woman's testimony.'

After the healing of the official's son: 'Then the father realised that this was the exact time at which Jesus had said to him, "Your son will live!" So he and all his household believed.'

Before the feeding of the five thousand: 'Jesus said to Philip, "Where shall we buy bread for these people to eat?" He asked this only to test him, for he already had in mind what he was going to do.'

And after that miraculous provision: 'Jesus, knowing that they intended to come and make him king by force, withdrew again to a mountain by himself.'

After Jesus debates at the Feast of Tabernacles: 'The temple guards said, "No-one ever spoke the way this man does".'

After Christ's words about being 'lifted up': 'He said this to show the kind of death he was going to die.'[3]

Here is the Bible expositor at work, before our very eyes.

This spirit of proclamation and appeal is woven into another device of Jesus' preaching (as reported by John). He constantly employs physical features in the created world to symbolise the reality of life lived in God. That is sometimes described as a *sacramental* approach; water, wind, wine, light, bread, are all invoked as images of the life that Christ brings (just as the religious festivals are invoked as symbols of that life). But there is nothing 'automatic' about reception of that life. The mere presence of water does nothing for us: we must drink it. The mere existence of wind achieves nothing unless we allow ourselves to be blown along by it. The wine must be

---

3. The references are 2:11; 2:22; 4:39; 4:53; 6:6; 6:15; 7:46; 12:33.

drunk, the light followed, the bread eaten. In one powerful saying this lesson is hammered home five times:

> 'If any man is *thirsty*, let him *come* to me and *drink*. Whoever *believes* in me ... streams of living water will *flow* from him.'

John himself adds his 'expository comment' to Christ's invitation, making the point two more times.

> By this he meant the Spirit whom those who *believed* in him were later to *receive* (John 7:37-39).

Sacramentalists, who love symbol and liturgy, understandably love John's Gospel because of these elements on every page. Evangelicals will want to reply: 'By all means value your sacraments and ceremonies ... just so long as you offer them as invitations to faith, and we mean faith in *him*, not faith in *them*.' As someone deeply committed to the saving message of Christ, I have no problem with symbols and ceremonies. Present them as visual and tactile expressions of God's truth and grace, not vehicles of it. Use them to invite penitence, stir up faith and invoke commitment – and I rejoice to know that in them Christ is proclaimed.

More – I rejoice to see the consequences. One Sunday morning a Hindu student, long hesitant about the claims of Christ, reached out for the bread and wine of Communion, and sealed the covenant between Saviour and sinner. I have seen many a seeker after truth only enter into the certainty of having found (and been found) when he or she submitted to the public testimony of baptism. I have no reluctance (when it seems appropriate) about anointing with oil in the hope of seeing a sufferer released into the caress of the Comforter.

The message behind the event

I mention one more feature of John's *proclamation* which has long moved me but which is rarely referred to in commentaries. The very writer who surprisingly passes over many of the great events in Christ's story (birth, baptism, temptation, transfiguration) makes profoundly spiritual comment on them.

There is no 'Christmas Story', but John tells how the Word took flesh and lived among men (1:14).

We read nothing of Jesus' baptism by his cousin, yet John the Baptizer offers the deepest insight to that unreported event as he proclaims the Lamb of God (1:29).

There is no record of the Temptation in the Wilderness, but we are promised that the Prince of darkness will be defeated (12:31).

There is no story of the holy mount, where Jesus was transfigured with glory and the Father's voice bore witness to his Son. But we have the assertion that the disciples 'have seen his glory: the glory of the one and only Son' (1.14).

No agony in Gethsemane is described, yet a few days before that event, Jesus is seen wrestling in an agony of submission ('Now my heart is troubled, and what shall I say?' 12:27).

There is no Institution of the Lord's Supper, but the Saviour has already declared the need to 'eat the flesh of the Son of Man and drink his blood' (6:53).

The extraordinary truth is that John is 'preaching' about events that he never describes. The events he assumes (from the earlier Gospel accounts and the oral tradition of the church). Their meaning he expounds as evangelical proclamation and spiritual homily. Here again is the preacher at work.

The evangelistic appeal

Not only does John report Christ's own preaching in far greater detail than do the others; not only does he add his own expository comments; I want to suggest that, in a sense the whole shape of the book is a pattern of preaching.

What shape is the book? I recall reading as a teenager my first-ever commentary on John (by Marcus Dods, second-hand shelf, religious, one shilling!). To my surprise that Victorian writer described John's Gospel as 'the most artificial book in the Bible'.

Words had changed meaning. To me, 'artificial' meant forced, insincere, a poor imitation of the real thing. Of course the writer meant 'constructed with artifice', 'skilfully put together'. He maintained that the famous 'Prologue' offers a shape to which the rest of the book conforms. He suggested the three R's of *Revelation, Rejection* and *Reception*, as an almost geometrical pattern.

'The Word became flesh and we have seen his glory.' There is *revelation*. God wants to be known. He showed himself perfectly in Jesus.

'He was in the world (but) the world did not recognise him.' That meant *rejection* (as I have heard a Scottish preacher say, 'He came to his ain place, and his ain folk didna welcome him'). But now the good news ...

'To all who *received* him, to those who believed in his name, he gave the right to become children of God.' What a liberating message for nobodies, rescued from the dismal downward drag of a God-rejecting world and brought into his family ... simply by welcoming him!

But does it in fact give shape to the whole book?

Sure enough, the threefold pattern repeats itself for several successive chapters. God's Son is revealed to the earliest disciples, to the master of the wedding banquet, to Nicodemus, to the much-married Samaritan woman, to the lame man at Bethesda's pools, and so on. The religious authorities are suspicious and unwelcoming, whilst the recipients of his self-disclosure find new meaning to their lives. The theme reaches a climax after he feeds the multitude with miraculously multiplied food (John 6:35-71).

'I am the bread of life. He who comes to me will never go hungry' – *revelation*.

'At this the Jews began to grumble ... "this is a hard teaching. Who can accept it?" ' – *rejection*.

'You do not want to leave too, do you?' Jesus asked the Twelve. 'Lord, to whom shall we go? You have the words of eternal life' – *reception* (John 6:35-71).

It is a thought-provoking and solemnising idea. I have known people discover a living commitment to Christ through having it pointed out to them. 'If this is so, I want to receive him now,' has been the response. I recall a passing hearer who accepted the offer of a pocket John's Gospel during an open-air debate in Nottingham market square. My address was printed on the cover. He wrote to me a month later, 'When I reached the part where Jesus says *I am the door, enter and be saved*, I believed, I entered, and I know I am saved.'

Can we discern a pattern to the book? Some see it essentially as the book of Seven Signs. It has been suggested that John's 'first draft' was exactly that: a booklet designed to encourage faith.[4] Others point out that most signs are followed by a 'discourse' (either a sermon or a discussion). The miracle of water turned to wine is 'applied' in a talk about water, Spirit, and new birth (chapters 2 and 3). The feeding of the five thousand leads to searching words about the living bread from heaven (chapter 6).

Into these sermons are sometimes woven the 'I AM Sayings'. Perhaps we should look for a pattern of *sign-saying-sermon*. This is suggestive and helpful. But the writer does

---

4. Scholars as different as Rudolf Bultmann and C.H. Dodd have favoured this view of a 'Book of Signs', or a 'Signs Source' which the Fourth Evangelist enlarged into his finished work. The 'Seven Signs' are usually listed as Water into Wine (2:1-11), Healing of a Nobleman's Son (4:46-54), Healing of a Lame Man (5:1-18), Feeding of the Five Thousand (6:1-15), Walking on the Water (6:16-22), Sight to a Blind Man (9:1-4), and Lazarus Raised (11:1-57). The number seven had special significance to Jews, symbolising 'completeness'.

not stick rigidly to the pattern. He is serving salvation-truth, not artistic considerations.[5]

The fact is this: although everyone agrees that the Fourth Gospel is shaped to speak its message, few can agree on the precise shape! One scholar has accumulated twenty-four suggestions![6]

Those who like a liturgical framework suggest that John has built his book around the lectionary (ordered readings and prayers) of first-century synagogue worship. Certainly, as we have seen, Jesus made powerful use of the temple festivals. His 'bread of life' discourse (which was partly given in the Capernaum Synagogue) certainly made use of the set-readings for Passover time (6:30-33, 45, 48-51, 58, 59).

This is not at all far-fetched. The highly trained Israeli tourist-guides are sometimes offered an extra course prepared by Christians, which links together the city of Jerusalem, the structure of John's Gospel, the ancient Jewish Festivals and the Christian Church Calendar![7]

---

5. The 'Seven Sermons' have been identified as 'New Birth' (3:1-21), 'The Water of Life' (4:1-42), 'The Divine Son' (5:19-47), 'The Bread of Life' (6:22-65), 'The Life-giving Spirit' (7:1-52), 'The Light of the World' (8:12-59) and 'The Good Shepherd' (10:1-42). They make splendid titles for a sermon-series, as many preachers have discovered. Notice how easily they can be adapted to sound more contemporary: 'Fresh Start', 'True Satisfaction', 'No sooner said than done', and so on.
6. Pryor, *John, Evangelist of the Covenant People*, p. 95.
7. With just a little stretching, the Fourth Gospel can be entirely fitted into the Jewish Calendar, and many of the themes 'match':
   1. Passover: chapter 1.
   2. Wedding Day: ('the third day', 2:1; favoured for weddings still today, because on the third day of creation God twice said it was good!)
   3. Passover (2:12 to 3:36): Lamb of God and New Birth.
   4. Pentecost (?) 'a feast of the Jews' (chapter 5): Healing at Bethesda.
   5. Passover (chapter 6): Feeding Five Thousand, (note verse 59).
   6. Tabernacles (chapters 7,8 and 9): conflict in the Temple courts.
   7. Dedication (chapters 10-11, note 10:22): The Living Water.
   8. Preparation (chapter 12): Unleavened Bread, Entry to Jerusalem.
   9. Passover (chapters 13-21): Upper Room, Crucifixion, Resurrection.

Other scholars reverse the suggestion, and propose that John shaped his book around a Christian lectionary, already in use among the Asian Churches. I find this an attractive idea, lover as I am of the Calendar (with apologies to my Scottish brethren!). Every indication confirms that the earliest Christians quickly adopted liturgy and 'common prayer', however distasteful that may seem to some.

My own simple suggestion for a 'shape' to the Fourth Gospel rests on the fact that a radical turning-point is reached at chapter 12. It is marked by the 'Palm Sunday' entry to Jerusalem, and the solemn, significant words that end Jesus' public ministry (in John's version): 'Having loved his own that were in the world, he now showed them the full extent of his love' (13:1).

My suggestion is this:

Prologue: God reveals himself in Jesus, the Living Word (chapter 1).

Part One: Jesus offers himself to the world (chapters 2-11. Most of the Signs, Discourses, I AM Sayings and Feasts).

Part Two: Jesus reveals himself to his disciples (chapters 12-20). The Upper Room Discourses. The Cross and Resurrection.

Epilogue: Jesus confirms his evangelistic commission (chapter 21). The final appearance by the lake.

Theology ablaze

Into this seemingly simple pattern is poured a kaleidoscopic cascade of words and actions, interviews and signs, festivals and sufferings. John presents the most profoundly theological picture of Jesus to be found anywhere in Scripture.

Reading John, I am reminded of one of the Anglican 'collects' (those mini-masterpieces of condensed prayer):

Almighty God, who wonderfully created us in your own image and yet more wonderfully restored us in your Son, Jesus Christ: Grant that, as he came to share our human nature, so we may be partakers of his divine glory: Who is alive and reigns with you and the Holy Spirit, one God, now and forever.[8]

Christ the source of our life ... Christ the only Son of the Father ... Jesus the unique revealer of the invisible God ... the Lamb of God, slain in the purposes of God to bring us all forgiveness ... The living vine, to whom all Christians are united in living experience ... The High Priest who prayed for us on earth, and intercedes for us in Heaven ... the phrases pour out, as we try to sum up what Jesus of Nazareth comes to mean to us when we take seriously the message of John. Here, truly, is theology ablaze.

Behold the wondrous cross

Like all of the Evangelists, John explores the wonder of the cross and the empty tomb. He does this in his own distinctive way. Mark showed with stark realism the suffering servant. Matthew explored the kingly aspects of him who 'reigns from the tree'. Luke, faithful to his brief, displays salvation and conversion at the cross. John paints his picture with pigments of mysticism, theology and evangel.

Jesus cries out his thirst; here is the subtle, ironic, two-worlds emphasis again: he who thirsts is he who alone can grant the living water of the Spirit. Christ's last cry recorded by John is not the dereliction recorded by Mark, but the '*Finished!*' of a work completed and redemption accomplished. When the spear pierces his side the 'blood and water' from a ruptured heart symbolised the two gifts of new life and forgiveness.

---

8. Quoted from 'Celebrating Common Prayer', Mowbray, 1992. Collect for Morning Prayer, Wednesday and in Christmas time.

> Let the water and the blood,
> From thy riven side which flowed,
> Be of sin the double cure:
> Cleanse me from its guilt and power
>
> (see John 19:28, 30, 34).

The Resurrection account picks up the earlier themes of witness borne (revelation) and faith expressed (reception). Mary, Peter and John see the empty tomb and the grave clothes and seeing, believe. Jesus enters the locked room and confirms these gifts of peace and the Holy Spirit promised in the Upper Room.

Thomas comes only slowly to faith, but when he gets there utters the highest confession, 'My Lord and my God!' Jesus appears by Galilee to 'replay' the scene of their first call and commission: his message is that his death has not cancelled out the commission for world evangelism; rather his resurrection confirms it (20:1-9, 19-23, 24-28; 21:1-9).

I recall being invited to speak to trainee Christian leaders on the subject of *Apologetics* (helping people to believe). I was asked to make the first chapter of John's Gospel my 'Base-line'. We examined together how in the first half of that chapter John produces his brilliant analogy of the *logos* ... God's eternal mind and purpose made known at a particular moment in a particular place as *Jesus came* ...

> Our God contracted to a span
> Incomprehensibly made man.

We then examined how the first five disciples discovered the man Jesus to be the person who precisely met their particular need and confronted their personal situation. To the friend of Andrew (probably John) he came as Saviour from sin. To Andrew he came as the fulfiller of promise. To Simon he brought the challenge of a changed nature, marked by a change of name. To Philip he presented the curt command, 'Follow me', for this was a young man who yearned for decisive leadership. To Nathanael he presented himself as the Way to God.

What they all discovered (I suggested) was that Jesus of Nazareth is the central reality around which everything else that clamours for our attention has to be judged and checked.

Incident after incident goes on to illustrate that fact, as others meet him. And, in those tense, pregnant, awesome hours in the Upper Room, those original disciples further explore what it will mean to abide in him, to trust in him, to find peace in him.

To underline my point (that this is still the purpose of Apologetics today – to confront real people with the Real Person), I listed from recent pages in my diary, some of the folk with whom I had recently conversed about the call of Christ to trust him, love him and know him. They included a middle-aged lawyer, a black-clad 'gothic punk', a young mother from the local 'mums and toddlers', a hairdresser emerging from a nervous breakdown, an unemployed seaman, a water-board engineer, a sociology student and a policeman. These people were no more varied than those vivid characters who walk out of the pages of the Fourth Gospel and tell us how they found new life in Christ. That (I suggested) is what Apologetics is all about and that (I now affirm) is what John's powerful argument is all about.

Bruce Milne has a sentence in the introduction to his splendid commentary *The Message of John* (an example, significantly, of expository preaching-in-print). I end this chapter with his words, to which I add a fervent *Amen*.

If Jesus Christ shares the nature of God we are called to worship him without cessation, obey him without reservation, and serve him without interruption.[9]

---

9. Bruce Milne, *John*, p.36.

So What Now?

Chapter 17

MYTHS, MIDRASH AND MAGI

I enjoy the detective novels of Michael Innes. Urbane, witty and literate, they follow the imaginary adventures of Britain's top cop, Sir John Appleby, or relate the strange commissions offered to that respected portrait painter, Charles Honeybath.

My sketchy knowledge of the art world (sorry!) is almost entirely dependent upon these slim tongue-in-cheek volumes. One thing I have learned is the importance of *provenance*. This is a concept related to the derivation, origins and ancestry of artistic works.

For example, imagine the appearance in an auction of a hitherto unknown Constable landscape. Where has it come from? It was discovered (we are told) in an attic in West Hartlepool. But no-one would accept that claim without checking its provenance. Is there any evidence that Constable ever contemplated painting such a scene? Any references in notebooks, sketchbooks, diaries or correspondence? Does some third party ever refer to it? Did the artist ever visit West Hartlepool (a far cry from his home in East Bergholt)? There is the matter of materials, too. Do the pigments used reflect the correct period? What of the canvas? The style? The subject? The treatment?

The most remarkable example of provenance I have ever encountered was in Jerusalem. A modern resident there dug deep beneath his house in the old city. He found, amongst other things, a 1946 'tommy-gun', sections of Herod's temple aqueduct, an oriental ring, and several arrowheads from the eighth century BC. Astonishingly, he established the provenance of all four items, the first from eyewitnesses, the others from Josephus, the Talmud and the prophet Isaiah!

I relate all of this to re-introduce the questions raised in chapter three. Now that we have examined each Gospel in detail, we are better able (I suggest) to answer some of them. How did they come to be written? What kind of message are they intended to convey? Can any clear line of connection be established between the events they describe and their commitment to writing? Did the authors use earlier sources of information or get it all out of their heads, so to speak? If the former, then were those sources handed on by word of mouth, or were some of them already in writing?

There are other related questions, too. We return to the issue of *genre*. Several scholarly writers have employed a gentle joke to pinpoint this important matter. The great Library of Alexandria in first-century Egypt was world famous. Imagine the head librarian receiving the donation of a new book called the Gospel According to Mark. On which shelf does he place it? How does he catalogue it? Is it Biography, History, Religious Studies, Myth or Philosophy?

I sympathise. A little book of mine relating adventures experienced and lessons learned whilst living in Jerusalem has turned up in various public libraries as Religion, Geography, Travel, Autobiography and Middle Eastern Politics. David Pawson's book on conversion, *The Normal Christian Birth*, once found itself classified as Gynaecology and Obstetrics!

Back to basics

Here then is a fundamental question. We hinted at it earlier (pages 31-34) but now return to it after taking a long look at these Christ-centred books. *What exactly is a Gospel?* It contains biographical material, but is not a true biography as we understand that word today (although it does resemble in some ways a first century *life*). It is undoubtedly historical, but cannot be called a history book, for the facts are too sparse, the interpretations too numerous, and the background information minimal.

A gospel is not unlike a modern 'documentary', giving selected information about Jesus of Nazareth, put together in order to create a portrait and convey a message. It has a strong element of interpretative comment. The writer is stating, in a vivid but subtle manner, what he himself believes about Jesus. You will recall that each successive writer spells that out, each in his own way, in his opening words. Mark's blunt opening 'This is the Good News': Matthew's elaborate genealogy that says 'Let me introduce you to David's Saviour-King'; Luke's lovely tale of angel choirs chanting good tidings; John's profound theological prologue; each is saying 'This is what Jesus means to me'.

A Gospel engages many of the attributes of *narrative prose*. It has a narrator who tells the story as he sees it, and as he wishes the reader to see it. Occasionally he adds an explanatory comment: this archaic word means that, this is why Jesus did that, this incident fulfils that ancient prophecy, and so on. In other words, a Gospel is essentially *a story*. As such, it has structure, plot, characters, tension, and very often involves the solving of some problem, or resolution of some situation.

The Gospel writer offers more than the occasional explanation or comment, however. *He interprets*. He is saying, in effect, 'This is what I believe about Jesus of Nazareth.' More than that again, he is saying 'This is what I hope the reader will come to believe.' And again more. There is a growing element of *doctrinal definition*: we are reading what the Church has come to believe, and should continue to believe.

Like Paul writing his epistles, though not so overtly, the Gospel writer is addressing particular situations. Luke actually names his first reader. Matthew virtually describes his type of reader (by means of his strong Jewishness). John clearly addresses readers who could afford to be clearer about the deity of Christ. Luke underlines the very lessons recently learned in the great Gentile Mission. Mark more than hints that his readers need to develop their thinking about undeserved suffering.[1] In all of this, the Gospels are at least approaching the point of a theological statement. Of course they do not compare with, say, the Epistle to the Romans or the Letter to the Hebrews in this respect. But they burst with theological statement. This is how the kingdom of God came, this is who Jesus is, this is why the Church celebrates Communion, this is the essence of the gospel. As Luke puts it:

> I do this so that you will know the full truth about everything which you have been taught (Luke 1:4, *Today's English Version*).

Fact or faith?

We could coin another phrase, and describe the Gospels as *faith statements*. But that raises a new issue. Does faith in the gospel message involve faith in the Gospels? Does the embracing of Christian truth involve acceptance of the Gospel record as true and reliable? Do the writers give us facts?

They certainly 'read' like that. They tell us things that happened and urge us to believe them. 'During the time of King Herod, Magi came from the east'...'John came baptising, and all the people went out to him'...'I have carefully investigated, so that you may know the certainty'...'We have seen his glory'...'We know that his testimony is true'...'We have heard, we seen with our eyes, we have looked at and our hands have touched'.[2]

This is of enormous importance in the search for provenance

---

1. Luke 1:3; Matthew 1:1; John 1:1-2; Luke 2:10; Mark 10:44.
2. Factual claims of the Gospel writers which I quote: Matthew 2:1; Mark 1:4-5; Luke 1:3-4; John 1:14; 1 John 1:1. Of course there are many more; they appear on almost every page.

(as I call it). The almost universal assumption of 'liberal' scholars (and, from them, of many preachers, most books and virtually all television programmes on the subject) is that the Gospels convey truth but are not true. A huge gap is created between facts and meaning, between history and interpretation. The four evangelists, we are constantly assured, are not concerned to give us facts, but to stimulate our faith. No-one needs to believe that wise men came from the east with gifts; what the story conveys is the truth that God's love shines on everyone and should elicit our response. No-one is expected to believe that crowds were miraculously fed; the moral of the story is that God meets our deepest hungers, and often uses our neighbour to express the fact.

The enormous attraction of this approach (and the real reason for adopting it) is that it removes at a stroke the irritating need to affirm the uniqueness of Jesus, the reality of the supernatural, and the claims of a divine revelation in the Bible. All of these Christian beliefs, held unflinchingly for nineteen centuries, are a thorough nuisance in the twentieth, because they clash with the current climate of opinion, which is a mixture of secularism and religious anaemia.

Introducing myth

We must pause and examine the word *myth*. This word, often misunderstood as a perjorative word meaning nonsense or untruth, is actually descriptive of a perfectly respectable literary genre. Myth attempts to express in the form of a story (with various accepted conventions) a truth that cannot easily be expressed in any other way. A lovely modern example of myth (I believe) is the cycle of Narnia stories by C. S. Lewis. There is no such place as Narnia, nor is there such a lion as Aslan. But the stories express some truths so powerfully that some children find it almost impossible to distinguish Aslan from Jesus, even though the books never spell out any connection between the two.

D. F. Strauss (1808-1874) described a myth as a symbolic expression or embodiment of an idea or a conviction. The Gospel narratives are, he maintained, examples of theology-in-pictures. The miracle stories, in particular, are mythological in that sense.[3]

Rudolf Bultmann (1884-1976) re-shaped and re-used the idea, but gave it a subtly different slant. To him, myth had to do with the way reality is perceived. In a pre-scientific age, people 'saw' mythologically. They thought of a three-decker universe, with heaven above, the underworld below, and the world 'here'. For us, knowing better, it is now meaningless and misleading to refer to God in spatial terms 'up there' (how far up there?) and of his Son 'coming down' for our salvation.

The much-promoted process ideal of de-mythologizing is the answer to this (we are told). This is not merely the stripping of biblical stories of their mythological clothes, to conjecture 'what really happened' (Strauss's approach). It must go on to ask what profound experience the disciples really had, which is both symbolized and expressed in these stories.

The reader will immediately recognise the kind of statement made by one now-retired bishop. What matters about the Resurrection stories is not whether they 'really happened', but whether you or I have a somewhat undefined experience which brings us to share the conviction of the early Christians that Jesus lives.

What are we to make of this? It may be a view promoted with sincerity and good motive (that of making Christianity more believable by requiring less to believe). But not for

---

3. See article on 'Myth' in *The Dictionary of Jesus and the Gospels*. I do not maintain that the mythic genre finds no place in the Bible, or is an unfit medium for inspired truth. I simply say that the Gospel writers were not offering myth, and would have been surprised and indignant at the suggestion that they were.

one moment should we imagine that this is what the Gospel writers meant to convey. Neither Inspector Appleby nor Charles Honeybath could be fooled for one moment, in that world of Michael Innes that is as imaginary as the world of the demythologizers!

The Gospels proclaim *the gospel*; that is, the glad news of God's saving intervention in this world's affairs, by sending his Son. We know God by seeing Jesus (John 14:9; Hebrews 1:1-3). The only Jesus we can 'see' is the one presented to us by the apostolic writers. They insist that he did and said certain things. They, and others whom they quote, were eyewitnesses. One of them, for example, spelled it out in words that are unequivocal in their meaning.

Peter, the fisherman and first apostle, was expecting soon to die. The church was well into its second generation. Some very peculiar versions of the Faith were beginning to circulate. Soon to be labelled 'gnostic', these ideas set little store by crude physical events, and valued mystical experience above all else. They were very partial to myth, because that was a useful form in which to express profound, exciting, spooky experiences, without any messy insistence on flesh and blood, pain and fear, love and sex, temptation and good behaviour. A psychedelic experience during a sacramental rite was much preferred to the hard work of reading your Bible and loving your neighbour. A shadowy emanation (favourite word) was more comfortable than a physical Jesus who got angry or sleepy, who touched lepers (ugh!) and who died in pain. (Some discerning readers may have noticed by now, not only the resemblance between ancient gnostics and modern demythologisers, but the danger that evangelical and charismatic Christians can fall into.)

What is Peter's reaction to all of this?

[You] are firmly established in the truth you now have ... [but] I think it right to refresh your memory ... I will make every effort to see that after my departure [i.e. after his

death] you will always be able to remember these things
(2 Peter 1:12-15).

He intends to put the record straight, by writing what he
will soon be unable to teach. Is this the first sign of Mark's
Gospel? Certainly it implies a written record of facts. Why is
this necessary? He tells us.

We did not follow cleverly invented stories when we told
you about the power and coming of our Lord Jesus Christ,
but we were eyewitnesses of his majesty (2 Peter 1:16).

The word 'stories' here is actually *mythois*, that is fables,
symbolic tales, myths. Peter is insisting that the Gospel Proclamation (soon to be recorded in writing) is couched not in
metaphors but in historical accounts of things that happened,
of which he and others were eyewitnesses. It is hard to imagine how much more clearly he could have said it.

In fact he does find one more way to spell it out. If any
detail of the Gospel record (apart from the resurrection) lends
itself at least to the possibility of being interpreted symboli-
cally, it is that strange occasion when, on the mountain, the
face and figure of Jesus glowed with unearthly light, a shining cloud descended, and the voice of God was heard drawing attention to his beloved Son. But Peter takes this, of all
stories, and insists on its physical and literal reality.

He received honour and glory from the Father when the
voice came ... We ourselves heard this voice ... when we
were with him on the sacred mountain (2 Peter 1:17-18).

What could be clearer? Christian truth is based on historical facts, attested to by eyewitnesses.

Learning from the rabbis?

There is another genre which must be mentioned briefly, for New Testament scholars refer to it increasingly. *Midrash* was a form of interpretation and comment much favoured by first-century rabbis. It was the attempt to give the Hebrew Scriptures (our Old Testament now) contemporary relevance by re-interpreting them in the 'today situation'. Closely related to this was the construction of *Targums*, which were comments on biblical stories with fanciful embroideries added.[4]

It was a method sometimes used by Jesus himself. Notice the surprising use he made of a detail from David's flight from Saul, and the unexpected application of Jonah's experience with the whale (Mark 2:23-27; Matthew 12:38-41).

Some liberal scholars have seized on this and suggested that many of the Gospel narratives are really elaborate midrashic targums. One goes so far as to propose that the whole of Mark's Gospel is an intricate Midrash on the first six books in the Old Testament! More modestly, others focus especially on the 'Christmas Stories' of Matthew and Luke.

I find this unconvincing. We have in the Qumran Scrolls some striking examples of Midrash. It seems to me that the Gospel records attempt in some places the *exact opposite* of Midrash.

Far from throwing Old Testament passages forward into (imaginary?) stories about Jesus, they throw the whole Jesus Story backward into ancient promise and prophecy, and say 'God planned it all along.' So, to the question, 'Do you think that Matthew and Luke dabbled in a little Midrash?' I reply, 'No, I think they told the truth.'

---

4. See articles on Midrash and Targums in *The Dictionary of Jesus and the Gospels*. In 1949, a hitherto 'lost' Targum was discovered in an ecclesiastical library in Rome. It offers some interesting 'details' of Cain's conversation with Abel before the murder! Again, as with myth, I do not deny the existence of something like Midrash in the New Testament. I simply say that the Gospel Account is not Midrash.

Chapter 18

THE GOSPELS AND THE WORD OF GOD

I want to return to my analogy of the imaginary painting and the problem of provenance. We have seen how helpful it is to think of the Four Gospels as four different portraits of one person. But who painted the pictures? How sure can we be that they are fair and accurate representations? How did they come to be bound in one folio, so to speak? Did each painter have a model or 'sitter'? Did he make preliminary sketches, which he then combined? Charles Honeybath would have done those things. Sir John Appleby would have asked such questions!

Of course the Gospels are not really paintings. They are word-pictures. So we ask slightly different questions. Did the writers make preliminary word-sketches? Did they incorporate into their work earlier writings by other people? Did Luke actually use some of those 'many previous attempts' to which he refers? Did he add his marvellous Christmas narratives (composed in a completely different style) because he came across them in an early liturgy, complete with canticles already being sung? Were those intriguing 'fulfilments' that Matthew loved to point out, already circulating amongst the churches, as a useful evangelistic tool?

Some basic facts

In the first century, writing was not done on sheets of paper, nor were there 'books' of consecutive pages. Sheets of parchment were covered with words, often without punctuation, and sometimes even without vowels. The sheets were sewn

169

together 'sideways on'. Reading several involved repeatedly
unrolling one side and re-rolling the opposite edge ... a rather
clumsy process. A complete scroll was stored inside a pro-
tective cylinder called a *capsa,* and an identifying label, a
sillybos, was fastened to the outside of the container. This
information usually included the name of the author; it was
considered bad taste to put your name in the script itself.

When modern scholars call the Gospels 'anonymous', they
actually mean no more than that. Very few books today include the authors' names 'inside' unless they are autobiog-
raphies or collected correspondence. Normally the name appears only on the title-page and the cover ... placed there by
the publisher. That is the modern equivalent of the ancient
sillybos. There is no reason to doubt that the earliest copied
Gospels were so labelled. Certainly the Four Gospels were
universally assumed in the early church to have been written
by the authors whose names they bear to this day.

The message preached

The Christian faith was first spread by the spoken word, in-
formally shared in personal witnessing, and more formally
preached in set-piece situations. Luke describes that double
activity in the city of Antioch, where the word 'Christian'
was coined (Acts 11:19-21).

The 'Bible' of these first witnesses and worshippers was
the Hebrew Scriptures, for Jesus himself had not only affirmed its authority as Word of God, but had claimed to be
himself the 'fulfilment' of that Word. Its content they carried in their heads. There was no question of an individual
Christian or Jew owning and carrying around such a vast
collection of scrolls! The Christians constantly quoted the
'Old Testament', as we now call it, in their evangelistic witnessing and their worship. The first Christian century saw a
stream of intelligent *pagans,* with no previous knowledge of
the Jewish Bible, and no conviction of its authority, coming

to faith in Christ because their attention was drawn to the Hebrew Scriptures *and thus to Jesus.*

Nevertheless, the Church soon began to value written words too. The Apostles increasingly discovered the value of preaching in one place, whilst writing to several others. The result was 'the epistles', several of which bear all the marks of 'preaching through the page'.

The need soon became obvious for written records of the original events surrounding the life, death and resurrection of Jesus. Old age or martyrdom increasingly silenced the voices of the only witnesses. We have no need to guess what they did to counter this situation. They tell us: they committed the facts to writing. We have seen what Peter decided to do and we have glanced over Luke's shoulder whilst he spelled it out to his friend Theophilus.

The idea could not have been new to them. It was at least implied in Christ's original call to them. He chose them to spend time in his company, to watch, listen and remember, using the method perfectly familiar to them, as practised by the rabbis and their disciples, involving both learning-by-rote and taking notes in shorthand. He then sent them out to share his message. Something else, too, of huge importance in the establishing of provenance; *he promised the coming of his Spirit to help them remember, understand, explain and record the facts.*

> 'All this I have spoken while still with you. But the Counsellor, the Holy Spirit, whom the Father will send in my name, will teach you all things and will remind you of everything I have said to you' (John 14:25-26).

Here is the first recorded hint of an inspired record, in which the witnesses are supernaturally aided. That is anathema to so many modern minds, but to ignore it is to ignore a whole area of evidence. To put it at its very least, the first

witnesses believed themselves to posses a divine commission and to enjoy divine assistance. As we shall see in due
course, those to whom they witnessed believed that to be the
case and only the case with the Four Gospels and the several
Epistles.[1]

Admittedly these words of Jesus do not specify Spirit-
aided writing. Admittedly, the apostles' immediate action was
to preach, rather than to write. But the promise surely implies both speaking and writing, since those were the only
two means of communication available! Moreover, it is precisely *in writing* that John conveys the promise of the guid-
ing Spirit to them.[2]

Believing themselves so to be called and equipped, how
did they set about the task? Much of the material was common coin in the early churches. Several thousand people had
been unforgettably engaged in some encounter with Jesus.
Over seventy had received a commission from him to preach
and heal. At least five hundred had seen some evidence of
his resurrection.

The apostles built both their evangelistic preaching and
their pastoral advice upon memories of the days when Jesus
was physically with them. Paul, a subsequent convert, gives
us fascinating hints of the enquiries he made of eyewitnesses.
He distinguishes clearly between his own best advice on a
tricky topic, and the actual words of Jesus. He records the

---

1. Within a great number of Gospel and Epistle references this implication of apostolic witness is worked out. Hence human testimony and
divine aid by the Holy Spirit go hand in hand. See Matthew 5:1; 10:19-
20; 18:17-18; 28:16-20; Mark 8:31; Luke 24: 47-48; John 14:26; 15:26-
27; 16:12-13; Acts 1:4-8; 5:32; 10:34-43; 1 Corinthians 15:6; Eph-
esians 3:4; Hebrews 8:6; 2 Peter 1:16-18; Jude 1:3.
2.'The two promises (John 14:26 and 16:12-13) do not refer specifically or exclusively to the inspiration of a New Testament Canon, but
they provide in principle all that is required for [it] ... It would be most
natural to believe that the promises of remembrance and of guidance
into new truth found their most far-reaching fulfilment in a New Testament Canon,' John Wenham, *Christ and the Bible*, p. 117.

institution of the Lord's Supper in the accepted catechetical formula, 'I received this from the Lord', meaning 'I was assured that this is what he said'.[3]

Were there any written records to supplement these word-of-mouth stories? It seems very likely, and Luke strongly implies this. He seems to have used material from Mark (which is scattered almost verbatim across his pages). Close observation reveals a lot of material common to both Matthew and Luke which is *not* drawn from Mark. This has led to the common but unprovable assumption that it comes from some document which is usually referred to as 'Q', from the German word for 'source'. The material has some common themes, and may well come from such an origin.

Most of the information would be in the form of parables Jesus told, brief sayings with which he brought incidents to a close, longer sayings made memorable by their rhyme or rhythmic construction, and colourful discourses on which subsequent preachers had commented and enlarged. The reader of this book will recall that Luke favours the first, Mark the second, Matthew the third and John the fourth.

The exercises of Source Criticism and Form Criticism reflect modern efforts to reconstruct this process, and if this is pursued with reverence and without preconceived notions of what is now unacceptable, it can be a helpful exercise.[4]

---

3. Paul's attitude to the record of Jesus: Roman 1:1-6; 1 Corinthians 7:10-12 (notice the contrast between 'not I but the Lord' and 'I, not the Lord'; the first is a direct reference to Jesus' words, see Matthew 5:32; 19:3-9); 11:23-24; 15:1-8; Galatians 1:18 and 2:1-2.

4. Source Criticism attempts to reconstruct the documents that may lie behind our present Four Gospels, and the oral traditions that preceded any writing. Form Criticism attempts to identify the shapes that these traditions and recollections took as they were passed around; parables, brief sayings, encounter-stories, and so on. It has to be said that the results are very patchy; the analyst tends to 'see' what his preconceived ideas dictate. If his starting point is that neither miracles nor prophecies can really happen, then he will automatically exclude stories of either from any possibility of being accurate.

At this point another factor entered the process. Each writer had immediate reasons for taking up his pen when he did. Each was writing into a specific situation. Each would be aware of some problem current amongst his readers. When Paul wrote a letter with this kind of thing in mind, he often began by saying exactly why he wrote. The Galatians were being misled by legalism, the Corinthians were engaged in party squabbles, Titus needed to identify leadership ability in Crete, and so on. The Gospel writers were less overt, because they were addressing a wider and more general issue; that of the fundamental facts of the Faith. But the specifics are there to spot. Matthew arms his Jewish Christian readers with evangelistic prophecy-fulfilment. Mark warns against a facile prosperity-gospel (thus anticipating the worst excesses of televangelists nineteen centuries later!). Luke underlines the importance of a truly Christlike approach to the dispossessed, the deprived, the sinful and those with the misfortune in those days to be women. John warns against the growing gnostic tendency to deny the real humanity of Jesus, whilst defending the church's flank against Jewish attacks on Christ's deity.

The modern exploration of this process also has a name; it is called Redaction Criticism, from the German word for 'editing'. This too is helpful, as long as the critic or analyst attributes honesty and integrity to the Gospel writers. But it simply will not do to assume that the original writer cheerfully bent the facts, altered the record, and put words onto Christ's lips which he never uttered. That would have been a pernicious habit at the time, and it is a pernicious habit to suggest it today. The editing, re-arranging and interpreting of the true events would only be a fair reflection of what really happened. Otherwise the constant claim to be witnesses to the truth is a lie and a deception ... as Paul and Peter had no hesitation in saying.

Did they believe it?

We must now return to the matter of *provenance*, and ask a blunt question. Is there any reason to believe that the apostles did in fact faithfully record the truth about Jesus? Is there a convincing line of evidence between the life of Jesus and the eventual appearance of the Four Gospels in an inspired Bible?

The answer is a firm and confident yes. First, a century and a half of Textual Criticism has established the remarkable reliability of the text as we now have it in our Bibles. The more facts that come to light, the more documents and fragments are discovered, the more confident we can be of the integrity of the material we are looking at.

John Robinson, hardly a conservative scholar, claimed with regard to

'... the textual transmission of the New Testament, the wealth of manuscripts, and above all the narrow interval of time between the writing and the earliest extant copies, make it by far the best attested text of any ancient writing in the world'.[5]

That in itself does not 'prove' that what the Gospels teach is 'true'. Spiritual truth is not answerable to laboratory tests. But it assures us that we are looking at the right words with the necessary provenance.

What we read in our modern Bibles is what the Gospel writers actually wrote. Within thirty years of the Cross, the written records were appearing. The oldest copies actually preserved to this day go back to within a century of their appearance.

To modern readers, accustomed to a world of instant communication, that may not seem very impressive. A thirty-

---

5. John A. T. Robinson, *Can We Trust The New Testament?*, Mowbrays, 1977, p. 36.

year gap and then another seventy-year gap? But this is im-
measurably better than the provenance of any other episodes
in ancient history. For example, Tacitus was a Roman historian writing around AD 100. The oldest manuscript we have
of his work *appears one thousand years later.* Caesar's *Gal-
lic War* (learned so painfully by so many Latin students) was
written around 55 BC yet the earliest copy is dated AD 900.

Similar startling figures contrast the number of copies
available from the ancient world. There are 20 copies of Tacitus, 10 from Caesar, and *at least 24,000 New Testament documents.* In other words, by the normal standards of historical
documentary evidence, the Gospel events are in a different
dimension altogether from any other series of events in that
world. To put it bluntly, if we cannot be sure of the basic facts
of Christianity, we cannot know anything about anyone from
classical times.[6] The New Testament simply stands alone in
terms of documentary evidence and integrity.

Into the wider church

The name 'Apostolic Fathers' is given to those church leaders who followed the apostles, and who either knew them
personally or met those who did. The rapidly expanding churches
were particularly careful to record who first brought the truth
to them. Names like Clement, Polycarp, Justin, Tertullian
and Irenaeus fill this period. One thing clearly united them:
they believed the Gospels to be what they claimed to be.

Polycarp (70-155?) was a bishop in Smyrna (today's Turkey). He knew the elderly John in his youth, and was mar-
tyred for his faith in extreme old age. His few surviving writings were crowded with Gospel quotations, references and
allusions. A frequent phrase, 'remember what the Lord said',
bears unconscious witness to the widespread knowledge of
Jesus' words.

---

6. Nicky Gumbel, *Questions of Life*, p. 25. He draws his facts and figures from F.F. Bruce, *Are The New Testament Documents Reliable?*

Papias (60-130?) was that likable if eccentric character whose witness to Mark we have already examined. He referred to Matthew's Gospel too, and gives the distinct impression that it was first written in Hebrew. This was a persistent idea in the early church. Jerome (fourth century Bible translator) actually records having examined the original copy, kept in Caesarea.[7] Modern scholarship has insisted for a century that the original was in Greek (as of course all existing ancient copies are). I have talked to Jewish scholars of the Hebrew University of Jerusalem who believe Papias was right; the Greek 'translates back' into very persuasive, well-balanced and rather poetic Hebrew.[8]

Justin, often surnamed Martyr because of his manner of dying, was the most famous of those intellectuals who leapt straight from paganism to Christianity by means of the Jewish Bible. He was powerfully engaged as an evangelistic apologist. I think of him as a Bishop Michael Green or Doctor Alasdair McGrath of the first century! It was he who described the Gospels as 'Memoirs of the Apostles', read alongside 'the Prophets' (presumably the Hebrew Bible in its Greek translation) at Sunday gatherings of the churches.[9]

Like Polycarp, this Christian philosopher both indirectly alluded to and directly quoted from many Gospel passages. He often described incidents from the crucifixion narratives, moving freely between the Synoptic Gospels and John. Sometimes he introduced quotations with the phrase 'In the Memoir it is recorded', and 'In the Gospel it is written' (notice the singular, not plural). Admittedly he never mentioned Matthew,

---

7. Jerome's reference to a Hebrew Matthew's Gospel is in *De Vinus Illustribus 3*. The tradition is very persistent. Eusebius the historian quotes a second-century Alexandrian churchman to the same effect. Origen, the colourful mystic, insists on it. See R.T. France pp. 60-66 for a helpful discussion.
8. Several Christian scholars in Jerusalem also now maintain a Hebrew or Aramaic origin for Matthew; see David Jackman, p. 12-13.
9. *First Apology* of Justin, para. 66-67.

Mark, Luke or John by name. Their supreme value to him is
that they bear witness to the one who has 'the name above
every name'![10]

Space forbids detailed mention of a host of other witnesses,
and I hurry to the final one. Irenaeus (born 175?) was the
outstanding systematic theologian of his day. He lived when
the Church fought on three fronts: against Jewish opposition, official Roman persecution and the soul-sapping con-
fusions of semi-Christian heresies and cults. His greatest written work was his treatise against Gnosticism, that mystical
experience-based, Scripture-twisting movement that threatened the Church's foundation (the New Age Movement of
the second century). Entitled *Against Heresies* Irenaeus' pages
are full of Gospel-based arguments.

Particularly fascinating is the way that he tackled the heretics head-on for their specious, selective, twisted misuse of
one Gospel or another. The answer to each, he maintained,
was to look at that Gospel whole, and in context.

So firm is the ground on which these Gospels rest, that
the heretics themselves bear witness to them. The
Ebionites, who use Matthew's Gospel only, are confuted
out of the very same. Marcion, who mutilates Luke's Gospel, is proved to be a blasphemer even from the portions
he retains. The Docetists prefer only Mark, but from it
their errors are refuted. Those who follow Valentinus make
copious use of the Gospel according to John ... but are
proved to be in total error by means of this very Gospel.[11]

His argument is very pertinent to our enquiry. The churches
that claimed to inherit and convey the apostolic gospel possessed the Four Gospels as we know them, and assumed them
to be what they claim to be. Even heretics can only make

10. *First Apology* of Justin, para. 1103-100.
11. Irenaeus, *Against Heresies*, Vol. 1, pp. 292 and 293.

headway by appearing to base their ideas on one or other of them.

Irenaeus brings us to the end of the era of 'Apostolic Fathers'. He got some of his facts from Polycarp, who was converted through the ministry of the Apostle John. The line is complete and unbroken. The four portraits of Jesus have provenance of a quality unknown to any other personal figure or any other body of writings from their era. There were four Gospels, and only four. Irenaeus felt this to be so important that he drew elaborate symbolism from the fact.

'It is not possible that the Gospels can be either more or fewer in number than they are' (he continues, in the same passage). He points to the four corners of the earth, the four prevailing winds, the four cherubim around the throne of God, and so on. To us the symbolism is fanciful, but the basic fact is solid. Those nearest to the appearance of the Four Gospels universally held them to be authentic, reliable, truthful, divinely affirmed 'pictures of Jesus'.

Chapter 19

BIBLE, CODEX AND CANON

The word *bible* simply means 'book'. Strictly speaking, there were no books until the second century AD. The scriptures were written on scrolls.

Then, around 130, someone had an idea. Why not sew the separate pages together only along one edge? Several could then be bound together between covers, with each page then instantly available without all that clumsy unrolling of parchment. With the title written on the spine, storage and access were both simplified.

The resulting handy volume was called a codex (plural, codices). One almost immediate result was the appearance of the Four Gospels bound together in one volume. It was simply called *The Gospel*. Each individual narrative had the words added 'According to Matthew', etc. The oldest surviving Gospel codex is dated around 130. The oldest one of which we can be certain was fourfold, dates from the early third century, and also, significantly, includes Acts. No-one now knows whether the invention of the codex led to the combining of a fourfold gospel, or whether the need for such a gospel precipitated the invention of the codices!

The next step was almost inevitable, and came within forty years.

An unorthodox Christian leader called Tatian unstitched the edges again, and re-arranged the pages to produce the first 'gospel harmony'. In other words, he tried to reconstruct one continuous narrative. That involved making some deductive or even arbitrary decision about the true order of events, since this differs quite strikingly at times in the separate Gospels. This famous *Diatessaron* (four-together) became virtually 'The Gospel of the Syrian Churches'. Its most striking feature was its use of John's Gospel as the basic framework, around which the rest was fitted.

In a sense, this was a backward step. *The four Gospels are meant to be four*: only with several portraits may the fulness of the Saviour's person and work be expressed. A 'harmony' assumes and expresses the historical truth of the Jesus-events, but obscures the distinctive witness of each writer. In general, the church could see that. The *Diatessaron* enjoyed great popularity, and was circulated well beyond the confines of the Syrian Church. Yet readers and writers continued to speak of a Fourfold Gospel as the definitive witness of God to his Son.

Heresy steps in

Almost simultaneously, a strangely attractive half-Christian teaching inadvertently contributed to the development of a true 'canon' of scripture. The word means literally 'list', but has come to mean more specifically a list of books worthy to be recognised as 'scripture'.

The heretic Marcion proposed a scheme which distinguished the 'inferior' creator-god of the Jewish faith (as he saw it) from the supreme God revealed in Jesus. Grossly exaggerating Paul's emphasis on the 'grace' of God, Marcion dismissed all of the Old Testament and much of the apostolic witness. To bolster his teaching, Marcion produced a one-volume 'bible' consisting of Luke's Gospel (with the offensively Jewish nativity stories missing) and the best known of Paul's Epistles.

Mainline church leaders responded to this mutilated canon by clarifying what they recognised as the true list, that is, the whole of the Hebrew Scripture (fixed by widespread Jewish practice well before then), plus all of the Apostolic Epistles and the Fourfold Gospel.

The Muratorian List (unearthed by L. A. Muratori in the eighteenth century) represents the Church in Rome's reply to Marcion. Added to it were some fascinating ideas about the origins of the Gospels. They perhaps tell us more about what the compilers felt should have happened than what assuredly did happen, but they give us the authentic 'feel' of the Gospels to readers living less than two hundred years after their emergence.

Luke is called Paul's doctor and legal advisor; he is said to have written on Paul's behalf. There is a naive account of John yielding to church leaders' demands for a written account, but only after much prayer and a confirming vision vouchsafed to his colleague Andrew.

Lists from other churches quickly followed. Occasionally one referred to 'other gospels', but these are never given biblical status. Always 'The Four' are unique. There was no unanimity as to the order in which the Gospels were placed. The Muratorian List suggest Matthew, Mark, Luke, John. Clement in Egypt preferred Matthew, Luke, Mark, John, putting first the two that began with genealogies. Others in Rome opted for Matthew, John, Luke, Mark (the two apostles first). Another preference put John first, either because of his theological profundity, or simply because of his opening words, 'In the beginning'. What mattered was perceived value, not chronological sequence.

Persecution and consultation
The rest of the story must be told quickly. The years from 170 to 303 were perilous but formative times. Waves of persecution swept over the growing church, as its wide-flung networks were seen as a threat to the stability of the Roman Empire.

Authorities learned to strike at two crucial areas of Christian organisation; its leadership and its written Scriptures. Churches sometimes responded to demands to surrender their

Bibles by cheerfully handing over pious books and apocry-
phal gospels; the pagans knew no better, and we, the distant
observers, are assisted in our understanding of 'which was
which'!

Meanwhile, with increasing clarity, church leaders were
identifying 'true Scripture'. At first the New Testament canon
was bound in two volumes, as Gospel(s) and Epistles. Eusebius, the church historian, spoke of the apostles having 'given
the Scriptures of the inspired Gospels in writing'.[1]

Of course few individual Christians had Bibles of their
own. Psalms were sung and Prophets were read aloud in
church gatherings. Gospel reading was given the highest pri-
ority (a custom still reflected in modern liturgies) and Epistles also were read and expounded.

After the official 'recognition' of Christianity in 303, the
Church rapidly spread and consolidated. Part of the latter
process was in the frequent calling of church synods or 'coun-
cils'. Modern Christians (and especially Protestants) can be
puzzled by this custom. What authority did such gatherings
have? What exactly were they doing when they tackled doctrinal problems, theological definitions, and (especially) the
biblical canon? Clearly, by their own account, they were not
giving authority to the Bible. Rather, they were recognising
and acknowledging an authority *which the Bible already had*.

John Wenham puts it succinctly in his book, *Christ and
the Bible*:

> Providentially, through the rise of novel teachings, the
> church had to ask herself afresh where the New Covenant
> was to be found. She knew only one answer: the apostolic
> church. And that answer was firmly grounded in the teach-
> ing of books already received as being of the highest au-
> thority in the church. The calling, training and commis-

---

1. Eusebius, *History*, Book 3.36:15, page 100 in Williamson's translation.

sioning of the twelve apostles was plain for all to see in the four Gospels, and the apostleship of Paul was clearly set out in his Epistles. Thus the criterion of apostolicity became paramount.[2]

In 397, the Third Council of Carthage, with Augustine present, listed 'the Canonical Scriptures, beside which nothing should be read in the churches under the title of Divine Scripture'. A copy of the list was sent to Rome, and this series of events is usually regarded as the first official statement on the subject by the church in the west.

Inspiration and the call to faith

All of this poses a vital question: How do we read the Gospels today? Surely the answer must be this: we read them as we received them; from faith and into faith. They are presented to us as truth about God's Son, to be welcomed with adoring trust. In them we read and hear the command and invitation of God.

In that mystery which we recognise as divine inspiration, we see God revealing himself in the experience of those who first heard the transforming call of his Son. They recorded and interpreted that experience. This they did, sometimes in response to immediate situations, sometimes in order to rectify misunderstandings, sometimes simply in order to leave the facts in the hands of those who would follow when they died.

Their choice of words was their own. There is in their writings no suggestion of divine dictation, of 'automatic writing' or of any compulsion save that of a passion for truth and for God. Yet they were conscious of certainty and authority.

Jesus Christ had called them, taught them and equipped them. He had promised them the aid of his Spirit, in remembering, understanding and explaining. Those two features (of

2. John Wenham, *Christ and the Bible*, p. 161.

eyewitness experience and authority to interpret) were unique
to them. Christians centuries later are not invited to 'remember it differently' or to re-interpret as they think fit, according to changes in the climate of opinion. New applications to
new situations there will certainly need to be. But reinter-
pretation is not something that we are invited, authorised or
equipped to engage in.

Such an attitude will make us more than a little wary of
'the sure findings of modern scholarship', when those findings (in reality, theories) come to alleged new conclusions
about the Gospel record. To regard them with a measure of
healthy suspicion is not to surrender to anti-intellectualism,
or obscurantism, but simply to recognise human limitations.
Scholars, like all humans, approach life with built-in presuppositions. If these include, for example, a dogmatic post-
Enlightenment assumption that prophecies, miracles and divine revelations simply do not happen, and that Jesus was in
every respect only a child of his time, then the conclusions
reached will be confused at best, and hostile at worst. Faith
(whether exercised by the Gospel writer or the reader) does
not come into the equation. But as faith is, in fact, an essential and required ingredient in the equation, the sum will never
come out without it!

Of course historical investigation, literary criticism and
so on can cast light on the context of the writing of the Gospel record, but that exercise in itself brings us no nearer to
(and no further from) our understanding and acceptance of
their truth. A scholar reading the Gospels is no better and no
worse equipped to understand their divine truth than, say, an
engineer, a plumber, a nurse, a housewife or (for that matter)
a Baptist minister! The apostle Paul puts it bluntly:

> We have not received the spirit of the world but the Spirit
> who is from God, that we may understand what God has
> freely given us. This is what we speak, not in words taught

us by human wisdom but in words taught by the Spirit, expressing spiritual truths in spiritual words. The man without the Spirit does not accept the things that come from the Spirit of God, for they are foolishness to him, and he cannot understand them, because they are spiritually discerned (1 Corinthians 2:12-14).

The recent Bishop of London has written (albeit in a slightly different context):

On the one side are those who believe that the Christian gospel is revealed by God at a time and in a place of his choosing, through events which are of significance for all time and for all generations ... on the other side are those who believe that the gospel should be adapted to the cultural and intellectual attitudes and demands of successive generations.[3]

Stepping out of the frame

This book represents an unashamedly personal reading of the Gospels. By that I do not mean an individual and idiosyncratic interpretation, but *an exploration based on personal faith, commitment and experience*. That faith, I maintain, is the normal faith possessed by millions of Christians spread throughout the world and throughout almost twenty centuries of history. It is what C. S. Lewis described as 'Mere Christianity'. The Christ of whom we read in these marvellous pages has become vitally and personally real to us, in life-changing encounter.

To take up once more the metaphor employed often in this little study, the Figure at the centre of each of the portraits has stepped out of the frames and become three-dimensional in our lives. He has beckoned us to believe and follow, just as he commanded those who first met him on the shore of Gali-

3. Graham Leonard in a letter to *The Times*, 15 June, 1990.

lee or in the streets of Jerusalem.

To some the call comes suddenly; perhaps even dramatically. To others (the majority, I suspect) it is more like a slow process than a crisis. The 'agent' may be a series of personal conversations with Christian friends, attendance at confirmation classes, or the invitation to an evangelistic mission. It might equally be a course of reading in apologetics, a visit to the Holy Land, or attendance at a series of house-group Bible studies. It may involve the impact of a personal grief, a growing sense of alienation or a profound experience of guilt. It might be sparked off by the personal witness of a new convert or the peaceful dying of a mature Christian.

The details are almost infinitely varied, but the outcome is astonishingly uniform. Within every church tradition, across every cultural barrier, within every century since Christ came, the authentic voice of Jesus has echoed from the Gospel writings, and struck a chord of penitence, faith and adoration.

Should I say voice, or voices? Matthew bids us view the One in whom 'the hopes and fears of all the years' are met. Beginning with Abraham, father of the Hebrews, his account ends with the proclamation of an authority that embraces every people-group.

Mark points to the perfect Servant, who trod the path of obedience through suffering, and thus established a kingdom in which the only sword drawn has the cutting-edge of saving truth. Starting with a man who proclaims new life, he ends with women who bear witness to an empty tomb.

Luke bids us gaze at a Saviour who sought out the marginalised and the lost. He begins with angelic visitors heralding good news, and ends with the ascending Lord stretching out arms of blessing over a prodigal world.

John cries, 'Behold the Lamb who takes away our sin'. He begins in a past eternity with God, and concludes with God indwelling the human heart.

Each Gospel writer makes his distinctive contribution to our understanding of what it means to be a Christian. Matthew calls us to learn and follow. Mark bids us take the path of faith and obedience. Luke reminds us that until Christ found us, we were lost. John offers a personal relationship with God, in Christ, by the Spirit.

The same deep merging of variety and sameness is echoed in peoples' experience today. The week I wrote this chapter, I talked to a Jew who related to me his discovery of Jesus. He was eager to emphasise that the call to Abraham was to 'bless many nations', and underlined it by reminding me of the opening and closing words of Matthew. I conversed with a young man who has pursued a path of servant-leadership that has cost him much, but has found expression in a Christian community made up of all ages, several cultures, and at least five races. He quoted Mark's most famous words (10:45). Someone has just described to me a newly-planted church in Europe whose large congregation is made up almost entirely of drug-addicts, half of whom have Aids. It is a model consciously based on Luke's Gospel. An elderly couple, frail, unwell, yet serene, have just described to me a life lived in the consciousness of Christ's presence repeatedly confirmed in the Sacrament of Communion and the hearing of God's Word. They were talking the language of John.

As I finish, let me use just once more the analogy of a portrait. The Church of the Nativity in Bethlehem is probably the building in Christendom that has been in longest unbroken Christian use. In the fifth century it was saved from destruction by invading Persians. It is a curious story. Bursting into the building to pillage and burn, the soldiers were confronted by a painting based on Matthew's account in which the 'wise men' worshipped the infant Jesus. With good precedent, the painter had dressed the magi in traditional Persian clothes. 'We are in this picture' cried the startled intruders, and, refusing to destroy the picture, they spared the building.

I have often told that tale at Christmas-time (sometimes in Bethlehem itself). I hardly need labour the lesson. The Incarnation only finds its fullest meaning when you see yourself in the picture. That is true of the whole united witness of the Four Gospels. From their varied portraits, a living figure emerges. But he will only be to us a living, saving reality when we are willing to step *into* the picture, and see ourselves there, gathered in adoration around the Living Christ.

Appendix

THE GOSPEL NARRATIVES:
A SUGGESTED CHRONOLOGY

Today certainty is not possible. As we have seen, the Gospel writers sometimes grouped their stories according to a theme, or in order to illustrate a point. Matthew and Luke provide a few clues, almost in passing. At their time of writing, there was no universal method for recording dates. The traditional reckoning of BC and AD was calculated several centuries later, and involved some un-noticed anomalies. The following suggested chronology is purely that of the author's. However, I owe several insights to the fascinating ideas of a Christian scholar resident in modern Galilee, Bargil Pixner, OSB, whose book, *With Jesus Through Galilee, According to the Fifth Gospel* (Corazin Publishing), I have found for sale only in Jerusalem and Capernaum.

The date of Jesus' birth
Matthew puts this during the reign of Herod the Great (Matthew 2:1-18). Herod died in March or April of 4 BC. Matthew implies that Herod did not live long after his massacre of children in Bethlehem. His final years, in contemporary accounts, certainly manifested the kind of paranoiac violence that the Gospel described. Herod himself set two years earlier as the possible birth of the child ('according to the time he had learned from the Magi' of the star's first appearance). All of this points us to something like 6-8 BC for the birth.

Two astronomical events offer possible explanations of the 'Christmas star' (which is nowhere said to be supernatural in origin). 7 BC saw a twice-repeated conjunction of the planets Jupiter and Saturn, the first time within the constellation Pisces, which was popularly associated with Palestine and

Israel. Around 4-5 BC a nova (new star) was sighted by Chinese astronomers. Although this was previously thought not to have been visible in the Middle East, more recent calculations have revised that opinion. None of this is decisive, but it could offer pointers.

Luke adds some facts, but they are not easily interpreted (Luke 2:1-4). There is no record elsewhere of Caesar Augustus organising a universal census. On the other hand, he is known to have been fascinated by tax reform and he reorganized much Roman administration. Egypt was the next Roman Province to Syria, the 'holy land' of Roman times. They had a census every fourteen years, and records survive from the one in AD 20. That would put previous attempts in AD 6 and 8 BC. Did Syria 'stagger' Egypt's programme?

Quirinius, the Syrian governor in Luke's account has caused a few scholarly headaches. He indeed governed Syria —but not as early as 'BC'. Josephus described a census of his in AD 6 (*Antiquities* 18:26) which aroused violent opposition, referred to in Acts 5:37. This date does not fit. But recent research has established that Quirinius had an earlier posting in Syria, as a local military commander. This was from 10-7 BC. Could he have set a census in motion that continued after he left—and which would later be recalled, fairly enough, as the census of *Governor* Quirinius—which by that time he was?

The second-century Christian leader Tertullian puts the 'Christmas census' in 9-6 BC under the Governor Sentius Saturninus. As he lived a good deal nearer the time than we do, perhaps he knew something that we don't!

A date for the birth of Christ is likely between 8 and 4 BC with the best evidence in favour of 7-6 BC.

The ministry of Jesus

Luke's clues, already referred to, furnish a rough guide, since we have independent dates for most of the people he lists. For example, Herod Philip had died by AD 34, and Pontius Pilate's governorship did not begin until AD 26. John's Gospel requires three years' duration for Christ's public ministry. All of this puts the probable date for his arrival in Galilee as AD 29-30, and the crucifixion as AD 32 or 33. Interestingly, several scholars, using different methods of calculation, have come to very much the same conclusion.

How old was Jesus when he died?
Luke describes his public emergence when 'about thirty years old' (Luke 3:23). John makes a surprising comment: only three years later he is described by critics as 'not yet fifty' (John 8:57). However, this was probably an idiomatic phrase: 'He claims to sum up the hopes of the centuries since Abraham, yet he hasn't lived half a century himself' (see the context of the remark).

Putting all of this together, the parameters can now be outlined.

Earliest possible date for Christ's birth - BC 8
Latest possible date for the crucifixion - AD 33
In that case he would be forty-one years old.

Latest possible date for the birth - BC 5
Earliest possible date for the crucifixion - AD 29
This would suggest an age of thirty-four.

Christ's public ministry - an outline
The Gospel writers were more concerned to present impressions than to organise a chronology. Mark gives a broad outline of the Galilee ministry. Luke fills out many details of a long tour of both sides of the Jordan valley. John refers to several periods in Judaea and Jerusalem. All mention visits to Samaria. Matthew and Luke speak of wide sweeps of preaching and ministry north and east into completely pagan territories.

John's frequent references to Jewish feasts provide an

outline of seasons, and this is strikingly confirmed by inciden-
tal references to weather and vegetation in the other Gospels
(especially Mark).

The following is offered as a rough suggested outline.

YEAR 1
January
Baptism of Jesus in Jordan. His first meeting with Peter and
several future apostles (Mark 1:9-20).

Early Spring
Having set up home in Capernaum (Galilee) he visits Jerusalem, demonstrates against misuse of the Temple, and gathers
disciples (John 1:28-3:21).

Summer and Autumn
After a wider Judaean ministry Jesus returns to Galilee via
Samaria. John the Baptist is imprisoned (John 3:22-23; Mat-
thew 14:3-12).

Winter
In Galilee, Jesus gathers 'the Twelve' and draws huge crowds
around Capernaum with his teaching and healing (Mark 1:14-
45). The Sermon on the Mount (Matthew 5-7).

YEAR 2
Late Winter and early Spring
First mission to Gentile 'Ten Cities' east of Galilee (Mark 5).
Rejection of Jesus by his hometown of Nazareth (Luke 4:14-30).

April
Feeding of the 5,000 in Jewish western Galilee (Mark 6:30-
44). 'I am the bread of life' (John 6). Probable visit to
Jerusalem for Passover.

Summer
Jesus sends the Twelve (perhaps earlier) and then the Seventy-

two on widespread missions (Luke 9:1-9; 10:1-24). He himself travels north to pagan Phoenicia and then south and east to Decapolis again, where this time he is welcomed (Mark 7:31-37).

Late Summer
Returning to Jewish Galilee, he rebukes the cities for their failure to repent (Matthew 11:20-30).

September
Jesus visits Jerusalem for the Feast of Tabernacles. He arouses controversy with his teaching and foils an attempt to arrest him (John 7:1-53).

October
Returning to Galilee, he engages in a brief teaching-tour. He then takes the Twelve north to pagan Caesarea Philippi and invites them to confess him as Messiah (Matthew 16). 'I will build my church.' The Transfiguration, probably on mount Hermon (Matthew 17:1-13).

November
Another brief return to Galilee, with a new emphasis on death and resurrection (Matthew 17:14-23).

December
Jesus and his disciples visit Jerusalem for the Feast of Hanukkah, engage in public controversy, and then retire beyond Jordan (John 10:22-42). Perhaps the raising of Lazarus at this time (John 11:1-54).

YEAR 3
Winter and early Spring
Jesus with increasing numbers of disciples travels throughout the Jordan valley (perhaps northwards on the eastern side, and southwards again through Samaria, Luke 9:51-62). This is the long 'journey to Jerusalem' described by Luke. Many famous parables (Luke 14 and 15).

April

Jesus completes his last journey to Jerusalem, via Jordan and Jericho (healing of blind Bartimaeus and conversion of Zacchaeus the tax-collector) (Luke 18:31-43; 19:1-26). He enters the city on 'Palm Sunday', cleanses the Temple for a second time, and creates a sensation for five days of public teaching and confrontation (Luke 19:28-48). He institutes 'the Lord's Supper' at Passover-eve, is arrested overnight and is crucified on Passover Day (Luke 22-23; John 19).

'The third day he rose again from the dead' ... 'he ascended into heaven' (Luke 24).

May-June

Six weeks later, at the Feast of Pentecost, the Holy Spirit descends and brings the Church to birth (Acts 1, 2).

Selected Index

Bibliography

This is not a bibliography for studying the Gospels. I simply list the books quoted in my various footnotes, and the works of reference which I used in preparing this book.

Needless to say, I do not personally hold to every one of the varied opinions expressed in the sources which I quote.

Reference Books

Dictionary of Jesus and the Gospels. Editors, Green, McNight and Marshall, IVP, 1992.

Gospel Parallels. A comparison of the Synoptic Gospels. Burton H. Throckmorton, Jr., Thomas Nelson Publishers, 1992.

The New International Dictionary of the Christian Church. Ed. J. D. Douglas, Paternoster, 1974.

The History of the Church. Eusebius, Penguin, 1989, trans. G. A. Williamson.

The Antiquities of the Jews, & The Jewish War. The latter 'newly translated and illustrated' ed. Galya Cornfield, Zondervan, 1982.

Jesus 2000. Lion Publishing, 1989.

Jesus of Nazareth, Saviour and Lord. Contemporary Evangelical Thought. Ed. Carl Henry, Tyndale Press, 1970.

A General Survey of the History of the Canon of the New Testament. Brooke Foss Westcott, Macmillan, 1875. (Out of print, but readily available second-hand).

Books Quoted or Referred to (in alphabetical order of authors)

Barton, Stephen C.,
The Spirituality of the Gospels, SPCK, 1992.

Blomberg, Craig L.,
The Historical Reliability of the Gospels, IVP, 1987.

Bridge, Donald,
Living in the Promised Land.
Jesus, the Man and his Message, Christian Focus Publications,
1995.

Brown, Raymond E.,
The Birth of the Messiah, pub. Geoffrey Chapman (Cassell), up-
dated 1993.

Brown, Raymond, E.,
The Death of the Messiah, pub. Geoffrey Chapman (Cassell), 2
vols., 1993.

Burridge, Richard A.,
Four Gospels, One Jesus?, SPCK, 1994.

Calvin, John,
Calvin's Commentaries (John), 2 volumes, tr. T. H. C. Parker,
Oliver & Boyd, 1959.

Carson, D. A.,
The Gospel According to John, IVP, 1991.

Clements, Roy,
Introducing Jesus, Kingsway, 1992.

Dale, Robert William
The Living Christ and the Four Gospels, Hodder & Stoughton,
1891. Ready available second-hand.

Dunn, James D. G.,
The Evidence For Jesus, SCM, 1985.

France, R. T.,
Matthew, Evangelist and Teacher, Paternoster, 1989.

Gooding, David,
According to Luke, IVP, 1987.

Gumbel, Nicky
Questions of Life, Kingsway, 1994.

Hooker, Morna D.,
The Message of Mark, Epworth Press, 1983.

Hunter, A. M.,
According to John, SCM, 1968.

Jackman, David,
Taking Jesus Seriously, Christian Focus Publications, 1994.

Juel, Donald,
Luke – Acts, SCM, 1983.

Lewis, Peter,
The Glory of Christ, Hodder & Stoughton, 1992.

McGrath, Alister,
Understanding Jesus, Kingsway, 1989.

Minear, Paul S.,
Matthew – The Teacher's Gospel, Darton, Longman & Todd, 1984.

Martin, Ralph P.,
Mark – Evangelist and Theologian, Paternoster, reprinted 1986.

McGowan, Hamish,
Personal Mark, Hamish Hamilton, 1984. Fount Paperback, 1985.

Marshall, I. Howard,
Luke – Historian and Theologian, Paternoster, 1970.
The Acts of the Apostles – An Introduction and Commentary,
IVP, 1980.

Milne, Bruce,
The Message of John, IVP, 1993.

Pryor, John W.,
John: Evangelist of the Covenant People, Darton, Longman &
Todd, 1992.

Ramsay, Sir William,
St. Paul, the Traveller and Roman Citizen, 1895.

John A. T. Robinson,
Can We Trust The New Testament?, Mowbrays, 1977.

Ryle, John Charles,
Notes on the Gospel of John, numerous editions and reprints.

Sayers, Dorothy L.,
The Man Born To Be King, Gollanz, 1943.

Smalley, Stephen,
John – Evangelist and Interpreter, Paternoster, 1978.

Vermes, Geza,
The Dead Sea Scrolls, English Translation, Penguin, 1994.

Warren, Norman,
On Your Marks with Journey Into Life, and Mark's Gospel, pub-
lished jointly by Through Faith Missions, Contact For Christ,
International Bible Society, Pocket Testament League, 1993.

Wenham, John,
The Easter Enigma, Paternoster, 1992.
Christ and the Bible, Eagle, Guildford, 1993.

Westcott, Brooke Foss
An Introduction to the Study of the Gospels, Macmillan and Co., London 1875.
A General History of the Canon of the New Testament, Macmillan and Co., London 1875.

Also by
Donald Bridge

JESUS - THE MAN AND HIS MESSAGE

What impact did Jesus make on the circumstances
and culture of his time? What is it about him that
identifies him both as a unique Saviour and the greatest example of gospel communication?

Donald Bridge challenges the way we view Jesus, and
our portrayal of him to the world around us. He ar-
gues that walking with Jesus today means reading
his words, welcoming the impact of his personality,
embracing the provision he makes for us, and sharing his good news with others.

Donald Bridge combines a lifetime of study of the
Gospels with an intimate knowledge of the land where
Jesus lived and taught. He has been both an evangelist and a pastor, as well as working for several years
in the Garden Tomb, Jerusalem.

176 PAGES   B FORMAT
ISBN 1 85792 117 8

SPIRITUAL GIFTS AND THE CHURCH

Donald Bridge and David Phypers

First published in the 1970s, when the Charismatic Movement became prominent in British church life, this classic study of gifts, the individual and the church has been revised and expanded in light of developments since then. The authors, Donald Bridge and David Phypers, give a balanced view of a difficult and controversial issue.

The baptism of the Spirit, with its associated gifts, is a subject which has perplexed and fascinated Christians. It is unfortunately one which also divides Christians who disagree over the extent to which gifts should appear in the Church.

Donald Bridge is an evangelist and church consultant and David Phypers is a Church of England pastor.

192 PAGES   B FORMAT
ISBN 1 85792 141 0

Donald Bridge is married to Rita: they have two sons and six grandchildren. He is a Baptist minister, now involved in church leadership consultancy. He has pastored three churches and 'planted' several others. Since 1972 he has also written or co-authored fifteen books of popular theology. His spare time interests include walking, sailing, archaeology, reading and stamp collecting.